T0370147

CONSENT

CONSENT

a memoir

JILL CIMENT

PANTHEON BOOKS
New York

Copyright © 2024 by Jill Ciment

All rights reserved. Published in the United States by Pantheon Books, a division of Penguin Random House LLC, New York, and distributed in Canada by Penguin Random House Canada Limited, Toronto.

Pantheon Books and colophon are registered trademarks of Penguin Random House LLC.

Excerpt from *Enormous Changes at the Last Minute* copyright © 1971, 1974 by Grace Paley. Reprinted by permission of Farrar, Straus and Giroux. All rights reserved.

The photograph on page 137 is by Jim Spellman/WireImage via Getty Images. All other images are courtesy of the author.

Library of Congress Cataloging-in-Publication Data
Name: Ciment, Jill, 1953– author.
Title: Consent : a memoir / Jill Ciment.
Description: First edition. | New York : Pantheon Books, 2024.
Identifiers: LCCN 2023041071 (print) | LCCN 2023041072 (ebook) |
ISBN 9780593701065 (hardcover) | ISBN 9780593701072 (ebook)
Subjects: LCSH: Ciment, Jill, 1953—Marriage. | Ciment, Jill, 1953—
Childhood and youth. | Teacher-student relationships. | Sexual consent. |
Authors, Canadian—20th century—Biography. | Authors, American—20th
century—Biography. | LCGFT: Autobiographies.
Classification: LCC PR9199.3.C499 Z46 2024 (print) |
LCC PR9199.3.C499 (ebook) | DDC 813/.54 B—dc23/eng/20231020
LC record available at https://lccn.loc.gov/2023041071
LC ebook record available at https://lccn.loc.gov/2023041072

pantheonbooks.com

Jacket painting by Arnold Mesches. Courtesy of the artist's estate.
Jacket design by Kelly Blair

Printed in the United States of America

FIRST EDITION

4   6   8   9   7   5   3

For Martino

There is a long time in me between knowing and telling.

—GRACE PALEY, *ENORMOUS CHANGES AT THE LAST MINUTE*

CONSENT

I

WHAT DO I CALL HIM? MY HUSBAND? ARNOLD? I WOULD IF THE
story were about how we met and married, shared meals for forty-five
years, raised a puppy, endured illnesses. But if the story is about an
older man preying on a teenager, shouldn't I call him "the artist" or,
better still, "the art teacher," with all that the word *teacher* implies?

The art teacher, whose drawings I had admired at his wife's gallery,
was surprised when I wrote my own personal check (I was sixteen) to
pay for the life drawing classes. I was flattered to be taken seriously as

an artist, to join an adult class with a nude model, a male in this case. I was still a virgin, and though I had grown up with brothers, the adult penis was something I had yet to get a good, uninterrupted look at. I looked that night, but I didn't draw it, though I drew everything else. The art teacher—gray temples, beard, my archetype fantasy of an artist—teased me about the blank circle in the middle of my drawing, but he also praised my innate talent.

The evening class had about twelve others, most retirees. They heard my story during coffee breaks. I planned not to bother finishing high school come May. Artists didn't need diplomas. I was an emancipated minor. My single mother had three other children to feed. She cried every time I told her my goals. With the money I earned from my part-time marketing-research job, I planned to flee the San Fernando Valley and move to New York City to become—no, to *be*—an artist.

I could tell the art teacher was impressed by my ambition. I could tell because he criticized my drawings as well as praised them.

Halfway through the semester, I caught him looking down my blouse, and that was more thrilling than the praise. I had been a late developer, and the breasts were new to me. No one wore a bra in those days—1970.

On the last night of class I stayed after the others left to get his advice about my upcoming New York move. He knew artists in the city who might need an assistant. In his private studio, adjacent to the classroom, he drew me to him, and I went willingly. I am purposely using the tired *drew me to him* because that was how my seventeen-year-old self (a birthday had passed), whose scant sexual knowledge came from *Valley of the Dolls,* might have described his action, and because to pull someone by physical touch makes him the aggressor.

Me too?

He was forty-seven, married for twenty-five unfaithful years. He had two children—a daughter my age and a son two years older. His once ascending career as a social realist painter had stalled, and he now sold commercial serigraphs his younger self would have found appalling.

He kissed me.

I could have screamed. I could have slapped him, but what seventeen-year-old is prepared to slap a forty-seven-year-old man she had fantasized about for the previous six months?

I fervently kissed him back. I had imagined his kiss ever since he looked down my blouse. But did I have the agency to consent? The teenage brain is impulsive. There is a mismatch between the limbic system, which is the center of emotion, and the prefrontal lobe, which controls logic and reasoning. California's age of consent is eighteen. There is a Romeo and Juliet clause in cases of statutory rape that forgives lovers close in age, but obviously that didn't apply here. Did the art teacher's behavior—the extra attention he gave me in class, the evening he used my arm to demonstrate how the tendons cross over the elbow, the night he looked down my blouse—qualify as *child grooming,* a term that psychologists use to describe a pedophile's recruitment techniques?

He had stopped wearing a T-shirt under his shirt after the weather turned warm, and I remember noticing how his newly exposed middle-aged neck sagged. I found it repulsive, yet I chose to overlook it. Does that constitute consent?

Near the end of the semester, when he and I were alone in a corner stacking drawing benches after class, he whispered (so the retirees wouldn't overhear), "I wish you were older." I had always wished I was older. I had wanted to be an adult ever since I was a child. "I'm old enough," I replied.

Was that consent?

I've written about this kiss before, twenty-five years ago, in a memoir about my youth, *Half a Life*. I was in my mid-forties when I finished the memoir, the same age Arnold was that night. The memoir is as close as I have to a transcript:

On my last night of art class, I dawdled in the hall until the other students were finished. I heeled the wall and watched them file out. As soon as they were gone, I slipped back into the classroom and shut the door behind me. Arnold was leaning against a window frame, arms folded, eyes shut, yawning. This time I approached him without a hint of coyness, without the spark of a blush.

I unbuttoned the top three buttons of my peasant blouse, crossed the ink-splattered floor, and kissed him.

He kissed me back, then stopped himself.

I had no precedent to go on except *Valley of the Dolls* and *Peyton Place*. I asked him if he would sleep with me.

He looked stunned.

I mustered all my nerve and asked again.

"Maybe we should talk," he said.

I shook my head no.

"Sweetheart, I can't sleep with you. I'd like to, but I can't."

"I don't see why not," I said. I honestly didn't.

"For one thing, I could be arrested." He smiled, trying to make light of things.

I had no sense of humor. "I won't tell anyone," I promised.

He put his hand on my cheek. He didn't caress me; he simply pressed his hand against my skin. "It wouldn't be fair to you."

The gesture felt so loving that I began to cry.

"Shhh," he said. He tried to take me around, but I kept my face averted. As much as I wanted to be held, I was embarrassed to stain his shirt with my leaky mascara.

"I bet you think I'm a big jerk."

"It's the last thing I think."

"I've made such a fool of myself."

"No you haven't."

"Do you still like me?"

He cupped my head in his hands. I could tell he was choosing his words with great caution. "Jill, if you were older, I—"

"I'm old enough," I said flatly.

I am sure Arnold said those words (maybe not verbatim but close enough) before he sent me home an intact virgin that night, as certain as I am that it was he who had been the instigator. When I wrote the scene (note that I use the term *scene*, not *memory*—scenes in a memoir are no more accurate than reenactments on *Forensic Files*), Arnold and I had been living together for twenty-seven years. If I had to rank our marriage at that juncture, I would have ticked the box "Very satisfied." The story of how a couple meets, who kisses whom first, who declares their love first, is as instrumental to a couple's mythology as a creation myth is to a society's ideology. The ownership of those memories is wrested back and forth between the parties (the bickering and talking over and cutting in that couples resort to when recounting their beginnings) until one of the parties dies.

Who kissed whom first? If Arnold kissed me first, should I refer to him in the language of today—*sexual offender, transgressor, abuser of power*? Or do I refer to him in the language of the late '90s, when my forty-five-year-old self wrote the scene? The president at that time was Clinton, and the blue dress was in the news. Men who preyed on younger women were called *letches, cradle-robbers, dogs*. Or do I refer to him in the language of 1970, at the apex of the sexual revolution, when the kiss took place—*Casanova, silver fox*? And how do I refer to myself? In today's parlance—*victim, survivor*? The words are used interchangeably but have very different connotations. Calling myself a victim would imply that I had been helpless, whereas calling myself a survivor would suggest I had empowerment. Or do I employ the language used to describe Monica Lewinsky—*bimbo, vixen*? Or do I talk about myself in the lingo of the sexual revolution? In that case, I was the coolest, bitchin'est chick on the block because I kissed my art teacher.

While writing a memoir, the time it takes to re-create a moment from your past is usually longer than the time it took to live the actual moment. The memory of writing the memoir slowly accumulates until it usurps the events you are trying to capture. It took me days to compose the scene. The kiss itself may have only lasted seconds. How am I so sure who kissed whom first, who was the transgressor and who the transgressed? Because I daydreamed about Arnold pulling me to him and kissing me for weeks, months afterward, longer than it took to write the scene. I know who kissed whom first.

There is another omission in the text. I promised Arnold that I would not tell anyone about our kiss, but in fact I did. I told my mother as soon as I got home that night. I was two hours late. She had just gotten off the phone with Arnold's wife to ask if there had been an end-of-the-year party. His wife had told my mother that she didn't know, her husband hadn't come home yet. I was furious with my mother for involving his wife. I told her that I was in love with him, that there was nothing she could say to stop me from seeing him again. She reminded me that he had a wife. I reminded her that she was seeing a married man, ten years younger than she, and (coincidentally) also named Arnold.

That scene isn't in the memoir. It would have been a compelling scene. My mother and I shared a bed because I had sold mine in order to turn my bedroom into an art studio. My father, whose side of the bed I occupied, had moved out—been thrown out—the year before. What writer wouldn't employ the irony of sleeping in your absent father's bed after trying to seduce your father substitute?

New York didn't work out as I had hoped—instead of the Greenwich Village garret I had envisioned for myself, I ended up in a squat on Avenue D. Instead of painting nude models at the Art Students League, I posed naked for "photographers" at a sex parlor called Escapades. But I was no longer a virgin. I gave that job to a boy my own age.

I lasted four months before taking a Greyhound bus back to LA. I returned defeated and ground down by the reality that just because I wanted to be an artist *really, really* badly, it didn't mean I would become one. All I had left of my aspirations was the memory of that kiss. I borrowed my mother's car and went to see Arnold. I didn't call first.

This is how I describe the reunion in my memoir:

Arnold's studio door was unlocked. I gave it a sham knock, a brush of knuckles, then stepped inside. He lay on his cot, asleep in a puddle of lamplight. His heavy square eyeglasses, pushed back on his forehead, doubled the lamp's glowing filament in miniature, like two magnifying glasses collapsing the sun to start pinpoints of fire.

I shut the door behind me and slipped the stubborn bolt into its rusty lock. Then I crossed the studio and stood over him. A book lay open on his chest; his arm dangled over the cot. A faint dusting of black hair silhouetted his forearm. He stirred, squinted up at me, and started to speak. I hushed him, touching his dry lips with my fingertips. Then I peeled off my ribbed T-shirt, lingered for a wooden moment in full lamplight, and lay down beside him. It wasn't hard to seduce him. The suggestion had already been implanted. My previous attempt, clumsy as it had been, must have tugged on his imagination until it unleashed tendrils of fantasies.

This scene is true in the sense that it has remained a consistent memory over the years. I'm fairly certain that it was I who seduced him that afternoon. But would I have if he had not kissed me first? Am I as delusional as Humbert Humbert when he narrates (Lolita is twelve at the time), "It was she who seduced me"?

In both scenes from the memoir, Arnold is passive, either lost in thought or asleep when I appear like a nymph in the forest. There is empowerment in remembering oneself as the sexual aggressor, especially after modeling at Escapades. But I don't believe that was my motivation.

When I wrote this, was I protecting Arnold? The statute of limitations had long ago passed.

Was I protecting my marriage? We had just celebrated our twenty-seventh anniversary.

I didn't ask then, but I have to ask now that Arnold is no longer here to sway or dispute me. Was my marriage—the half century of intimacy, the shifting power, the artistic collaborations, the sex, the shared meals, the friends, the travels, the illnesses, the money worries, the houses, the dogs—fruit from the poisonous tree?

2

THE POINT OF VIEW IN A MEMOIR IS CURIOUS. THE WRITER MUST
trick the reader (and herself) into believing that she actually remem-
bers how she felt decades ago. A memoir is closer to historical fiction
than it is to biography. And as with historical fiction, the reader often
learns more about the period in which the book was written than the
period that is being written about.

The memoir was my third book, written in the early '90s. I wrote it
because I was worried that my actual childhood would be annihilated
by my fictional childhood, and because I needed to see if I had the
nerve to step out from behind the curtain.

Arnold and I lived on the eastern hip of Manhattan—Loisaida (if
you were a local), Alphabet City (if you were looking to buy drugs), or
the East Village (if you were looking to sell real estate). Our apartment
was a fourth-floor walk-up on 7th Street between Avenue C and the
projects. It was the only block in the neighborhood that had not been
razed by *Jewish lightning,* the local euphemism for arson and insurance
fraud. Squatters had assembled in the ruins. Homeless had built a cardboard city in Tompkins Square Park. As I walked down my block, I

would hear "Hometown girl, hometown girl," a refrain from the drug dealers announcing that I was a local and not a buyer.

I taught as an adjunct at three different universities coincidentally three hours apart. On Mondays, I gave three back-to-back identical three-hour lectures on Western civilization. On Tuesdays, I taught a fiction-writing workshop in Brooklyn, then took a commuter train upstate to run a nonfiction workshop in the evening. Wednesday was prep. I read Plato for the first time, one symposium ahead of the students, and student stories about hamsters falling in love and chimpanzees that lose their tails, even though chimpanzees don't have tails. On Thursdays, I lectured on what I could remember of Plato's lecture on Eros without confusing it with the hamsters.

I was the only sugar baby I knew who lived with a sugar daddy without sugar.

He was seventy-one when I began the memoir, seventy-five when I finished it. During the four years it took me to re-create my hard-scrabble childhood with enough swagger that the reader didn't feel sorry for me, Arnold had suffered pneumonia twice; a cataract surgery that nearly blinded him; a prostate infection that was only controlled, never cured; a debilitating case of shingles; and postherpetic neuralgia that made ascending the four flights of stairs with groceries—and a dachshund who had to be carried—as complicated as supplying base camp at Everest. Yet there is no foreshadowing in the memoir of what was to become of us, with one striking exception.

> He intimated there was something I didn't grasp [about our future], a demise, an inevitable end, a sorrow I couldn't imagine.

He knew what was to become of us.

One day, as we sat on a park bench in Tompkins Square, a homeless woman approached us. The park had been the scene of riots only a few years before when police, under Mayor Giuliani's command, had bulldozed the homeless residents' tents and refrigerator boxes. It was March, unseasonably cold. Arnold and I had taken the day off to celebrate my birthday (forty-four) with margaritas at lunch. We were both a little tipsy. We would have liked to snuggle against the cold, but the city had put iron dividers across the park benches so that the homeless, who had nowhere else to go, now had nowhere to lie down.

As Arnold fell asleep, his white hair lifted in the wind, his jaw slackened, his chin sank to his chest.

"Can I ask you something?" the homeless woman said. "How much do you get paid to take care of him?"

3

WHEN ARNOLD DIDN'T PHONE ME AFTER WE HAD SEX THAT FIRST time, it never occurred to me that he might be scared witless to call me at my mother's house. After one week of silence, I lost my appetite. Week two, I lost my ability to sleep.

Plato describes the physical transformations a soul experiences after being pierced by Eros's arrow: "The shoulder blades which up until now have been rigid, melt open, and small wings begin to swell and grow from the root upwards. Like a child whose teeth are just starting to grow in, the gums are all aching and tingling—that is exactly how the soul feels when it begins to grow wings." But when your beloved fails to phone you after three weeks, the soul feels like a child whose budding teeth have been knocked out.

Finally, a letter from Arnold arrived.

The letter was typed and formatted in the semi-block style that my old typing teacher had taught us to use for a less formal business tone.

September 17, 1970
Dear Jill,

Are you __ever__ coming back to class? Please call.
All the best, Arnold

Composing that letter must have taken him more than one try. The words, after all, must not alarm the mother should she open it, while at the same time lure the daughter.

He must have written it in his studio. He wouldn't dare write it at home with his wife nearby. So, he was in his studio, surrounded by the unsold paintings from his former glory days. The day cot where we had sex was adjacent to his desk. The sheets most likely had not been changed. He wouldn't take them home for his wife to wash.

Even after more than four decades of marriage to him, try as I might, I cannot imagine how he was justifying his behavior to himself. Was he telling himself that a seventeen-year-old had bewitched him? Keep in mind, a month had passed and he had not heard from me. Perhaps I had changed my mind or come to my senses? Perhaps my mother had found out?

A forty-seven-year-old art teacher mailing a love letter in the guise of an educational solicitation to his teenage student is creepy—more than creepy, sinister. Yet the memoir treats the episode comically, a missive between star-crossed lovers.

(Sinister or amusing? There are three Jills weighing in: the agonized teenager crying in frustration because she can't decipher nuance in an adult's letter; the forty-four-year-old memoirist, entertained by her younger self's confusion and Arnold's predicament; and me, the one who knows how the story ends.)

That afternoon, I reread Arnold's letter obsessively, but I could not crack its meaning. At seventeen, I could not conceive that he might be wary to write a frank and open letter about our sexual tryst and mail it to my mother's house. I was not sure whether he was hinting that I should call him or if he just wanted me to return to class, be his mere student again, and that wounded me more deeply than his not calling me in the first place.

I did not call him.

He called me.

When Arnold phoned a couple of days later on the guise of a follow-up to his letter, he kept up the ruse until he realized it was me on the line, then wanted to know when he could see me.

I sped to his studio. (I still didn't understand the reason for all the subterfuge.) The fact that he had a wife and kids—even the concept of a wife and kids—was unreal to me, a disposable black-and-white, two-dimensional family that came with every dime-store picture frame.

I opened his door without knocking. He was sitting on his cot wearing a fresh white T-shirt. His khakis, socks, and shoes still held a splattering of the day's paint, as if they'd been cut from a single bolt of smears. I acted all casual, glancing at the unfinished canvas. I did the squint, take a step backward, cock the head routine I'd seen in galleries. But when he stood up and put his arms around me, I started to cry. I tried to turn away, but he held me against him.

"What is it?" he asked. "What's wrong?"

I pressed my brow against the eye-frying white of his T-shirt. I said, "I didn't think you were ever going to call."

"Jill, I felt preposterous phoning your mother's house. I—" He cupped my head in his hands. "I didn't know if you wanted me to. Why didn't you call me?"

The memoir breezes over the disturbing fact that Arnold did not wait for me to "please call" as his letter suggested. He called me. He not only wrote a solicitation to an underage girl; when he didn't hear back from the girl, he called her.

There is one last detail the memoir gets wrong. In the scene, I dressed him in an "eye-frying white" T-shirt. He never wore T-shirts except under his shirts and only when the weather was cold. I have done the research—October 17, 1970, was too hot for him to have worn a T-shirt under his shirt. Would the scene read differently if I had dressed him differently? *I opened his door without knocking. He was sitting on his cot wearing an open shirt. I remember noticing how his newly exposed middle-aged neck sagged. I found it repulsive, yet I chose to overlook it.*

When we lay down on the soiled sheets to have sex, he didn't get an erection right away. I didn't know if this was normal for a middle-aged man or if his lack of readiness had something to do with me. The boy I lost my virginity to always had an erection *before* he took off his underwear. Arnold suggested I put his penis in my mouth to help him get hard. When my lack of technique made it obvious that I had never done this before, he instructed me on what he liked.

I only bring up the oral lesson to make a point. The power he once held over me—his ability (in my mind) to anoint me an artist—now shifted to a different kind of power: carnal knowledge. He had the knowledge and I wanted it.

4

WHEN I WAS NOT LEARNING ABOUT FELLATIO FROM ARNOLD, I
was sleeping on my father's side of the bed. The memoir never mentions the unresolved Oedipus complex or any other daddy issues. To
mention the Oedipus complex, I believed, would have been stating the
obvious, an insult to the reader who might not have read Freud but
who had certainly heard of the complex.

I no longer believe in withholding something just because it is obvious. Clichés become clichés because they are true.

He is old enough to be her father.

My own father was living in the San Fernando Valley, at the Mon-
tego Arms, a studio-apartment complex as nondescript as a cardboard
box. The year before, my mother had told him she wanted a divorce.
When he refused to leave, my older brother, Jack, had to physically
push him out the front door. He got as far as the end of the driveway, where he camped in his car for days afterward hoping my mother
would change her mind.

Today, my father would be diagnosed as "on the spectrum." But in
the late '60s there was no spectrum. All we knew was that he did not
like to touch or be touched, he didn't like to bathe or change his under-

wear, he wouldn't share his food, and he combusted into rage when one of us kids did anything that cost money—like break a finger or need shoes. When the memoir was published, an old neighbor whose children I babysat as a teen wrote me to say that even after twenty-five years she still remembered my father screaming.

Say there was no fresh fruit in the house. He'd stand before the open fridge, blanched by its glacial light, and stare at—no, fixate on—the plastic bin where fruit should have been.

"Okay, what happened to my peaches? What happened to the goddamn peaches? This is my house. My house. There should be peaches waiting for me when I get home. Sure, sure, the kids ate the peaches. Lord high-and-mighty Jack does nothing around here, doesn't do a goddamn thing to help his father, but he eats his father's peaches. Does she [my mother] care? Noooooo. She probably encourages the kids. She probably hides peaches all over their goddamn rooms. Why the hell can't there be peaches?"

I spend pages in the memoir describing my father's furies, but I never mention the other look he gave me. I saw that same look when I visited a friend who was in the late stages of Alzheimer's. She had no idea who I was but pretended to recognize me. At the same time, she was suspicious as to why a stranger was in her house.

That was how my father saw me.

In December, Arnold and I took a road trip up the California coast. It was only for a week, but once I had spent the entire night with him, nothing less would do. This is how the memoir describes our first vacation:

We traveled from motel to boggy motel, each a damp block or two from the gray Pacific. Most of the rooms had yellow blinds or yellow curtains, a trick to make the weary traveler believe every morning is filled with sunny skies and bright hopes. I cried mostly at dawn, shut in the bathroom, a nubby towel monogrammed with CARMEL HOLIDAY or JOLLY ROGER'S INN crushed against my eyes, while Arnold stood outside the locked door, on the cold linoleum, asking what was wrong. We both knew. I couldn't bear his being married any longer.

One morning, after a particularly melodramatic jag of tears, I came out of the bathroom and found him standing by the window. He looked exhausted, having spent most of the night trying to comfort me. It was 5:00, maybe 6:00 A.M. The room was suffused in red, save for the yellow blinds. They cast an especially false, garish light. He had wrapped himself in a pilled pink bedspread. His hair wasn't combed and the coarse gray, far thicker than the fine black, spiked out in all directions. His eyeglasses stood abandoned on the nightstand and he seemed totally lost, a middle-aged man watching the day break or the world end in a gaudy yellow flash, and I knew then that there was no one I would ever love more.

Could I have felt so sure of my love at seventeen that I knew nothing would surpass it? Or was my forty-five-year-old self, in the middle of the marriage and the memoir, trying to burnish the story with love lest it read like a reenactment of Humbert Humbert and Lolita's cross-country road trip?

At one of the boggy motels, I got my period while we were having sex.

Only in the morning light did we see the blood—blood on the sheets, blood on the pillows, a bloody handprint (his) on the wall. Outside, we heard the maid's cart trundle closer. We decided to make a run for it, but Arnold's VW wouldn't start. He got out to push, while I slid behind the wheel to gas the accelerator and ignite the engine when we got up to speed.

The maid stopped to watch the middle-aged man push the vehicle out of the parking lot into traffic with the teenager behind the wheel. Then she unlocked our door and rolled her cart into what must have looked like the scene of a crime. What could she have thought?

He is old enough to be her father.

5

WE HAD SEX IN THE PARK NEAR HIS STUDIO ON MORE THAN ONE occasion. In the memoir, I describe the park as "no wider than a bowling alley" without mentioning that I practiced fellatio on him in the tall grass. Wedged between Santa Monica Boulevard and Barton Way, the park was more a center divider than a pastoral setting. Its foliage had been designed to look sumptuous from a speeding vehicle, but to a crawling Beverly Hills patrol car with a suspicious spotlight, the tall grasses and queen palms were not especially concealing.

One evening, a beam of light crossed us. I froze, held my breath until the beam moved on. Arnold did not lose his erection and that surprised me. In his studio, he lost his erection anytime the phone rang.

Instead, he got harder in my mouth.

———

Arnold was in psychoanalysis at the time, as were most of his comrades—lapsed communists with successful fur businesses, screenwriters who yearned to write novels, and admen who wished they were artists. These were the days before pharmacological fixes, so no one had any choice but to talk and talk and talk until the demons got bored and left on their own. Therapy, like communism, was an evangelical passion, and Arnold was no exception. Since I couldn't afford psycho-analysis, he became my de facto therapist.

After sex, he might ask, "How did it make you feel when your father screamed?"

Or: "What do you think the ladder in your dream means?"

Or: "It's important to find and identify unhealthy patterns in your past, Jill, otherwise you'll be doomed to repeat them. You said that you unconsciously berate yourself for not succeeding in New York. Do you see a pattern there?"

Next, he might instruct me to tug at a memory from the web of my childhood until I could see how it was attached to the rest of my life.

No one had ever shown any interest in my "patterns" before, not even me. No one had ever asked me about my past. My contemporaries and I asked questions of each other all the time, but only about our futures. Arnold asked me about my childhood because—let us be clear—it was the only past I had. When someone asks you about your future, it is make-believe, science fiction. But when someone asks you about your past, your story becomes a mystery. Having a secret that someone else wants is powerful. I began to see how I could control his attention not just with my body but with my mind. I could not have imagined anything more erotic.

Twice a week he saw his analyst, a woman who practiced a mix of Jungian, gestalt, and horse sense. I was the subject of more than one therapy session. I knew because he and I would discuss his sessions, hunting for patterns in his childhood and youth and twenty-six-year marriage: He grew up during the Great Depression, he never got a childhood, he married too early, his mother sent him a birthday card that read, *If it wasn't your birthday, I'd tell you how I'm really feeling.* Could any of these be the reason he couldn't tell his wife he was leaving her for a teenager?

Or maybe his analyst asked him about the other sources of his anxiety besides me. His wife, of course. And his other mistress, E.

I knew about E. He had promised me that he was going to break up with her soon, but it was complicated. She was married to a friend of his. The two couples dined regularly together. The affair had started seven years ago when E took private drawing lessons with him, though he assured me, she was not nearly as talented as I. I accepted his Gordian sex life as the birthright of the male artist.

But I was curious.

"Do you still have sex with your wife?"

"I have to, Jill, or she would be suspicious."

"What about E?"

"I've only made love to her once since I started seeing you."

"Isn't she suspicious?"

E, by the way, never made it into the memoir.

6

A NUMBER OF RESTAURANTS ARE MENTIONED IN THE MEMOIR but not this one.

Ah Fong's was dark and smoky and "Oriental," not so much Chinese as Hollywood Chinese: opium eaters and white slave girls and red lanterns in tales from the exotic East. Arnold and I dined there most evenings after sex, so it is curious that Ah Fong's never makes an appearance.

Was I worried that if I set a scene with such a backdrop, I might give the reader the wrong impression?

It is one thing to place a middle-aged man and a teenager across a booth in a brightly lit Bob's Big Boy or Four-and-Twenty Pies and quite another to sketch for the reader the image of an older man escorting a teenage girl—flush with sex—past a mirrored tiki bar into a dark private booth in the rear of a restaurant.

Ah Fong's was downstairs from his studio in a three-story Spanish-style building that was a throwback to Beverly Hills's quainter days. The landlord had won the building in a poker game during the Depression and rented the top two floors to artists and screenwriters for cost.

The maître d', a thin Taiwanese man who always wore a tuxedo, knew Arnold by name and always sat us in the same discreet booth. Arnold taught me how to use chopsticks and which appetizer to dip into which sauce. The oldest waiter I had ever seen would appear out of nowhere to take our order, but it was only a formality. He already knew what Arnold liked and how to prepare the dishes.

He always brought Arnold a vodka martini, straight up, with two olives, and me a Coke.

One evening, between the egg drop soup and the wild plum chicken, Arnold told me that he had fallen in love with me.

I did not say *I love you* back. Declaring love for someone other than my family seemed a bigger rupture between childhood and adulthood than losing my virginity.

I didn't say *I love you* back—I was struck mute—but had I said it, could I have meant the same emotion as Arnold? Is love, erotic love—what Plato called the "divine madness"—an emotion? *Emotion* is a relatively recent term. Historically, people spoke not of emotions but of passions when they spoke about erotic love, feelings so compelling and intoxicating that they are beyond our control.

I believe Arnold was experiencing feelings beyond his control when he declared his love for me. But was I? Or was I seeing myself for the first time reflected in his desire; was the love I was experiencing for him or for myself?

New Year's Eve. We had been seeing each other for four months if you count the month he was too scared to call the house. Our affair was a secret (he made me promise) except that I had already told my mother and brothers that if Arnold phoned pretending to be Sheldon (a name I picked), they must give me the message. Even my mother had to laugh.

Should I be calling it *our* affair? Wasn't it *his* affair? When a seventeen-year-old dated someone exclusively in those days—it was still 1970 until midnight—she wasn't having an affair; she was going steady.

The seniors at my high school (the class I would have graduated with had I not dropped out) still practiced the ritual of going steady. The boy gave the girl a visible token of his commitment—a letterman jacket, a birthstone ring, a slave anklet. Exclusivity began after that. The boy was expected to call the girl a certain number of times a week and take her on a certain number of dates per week. Neither party was allowed to pay too much attention to anyone of the opposite sex, let alone date someone else (or be married to someone else, as in my case). Sex transitioned from first base (kissing and caresses above the neck) to second base (kissing and caresses above the waist) to third base (kissing and caressing below the waist) to home run.

Arnold was having an affair.

I was going steady.

When he told me that he couldn't see me on New Year's Eve, I said no big deal, I had plans anyway. Except I didn't. When a boy and girl went steady, it meant a guaranteed date for New Year's Eve.

I spent the evening with my mother and brothers eating TV dinners and watching the ball drop in Times Square, only two blocks away from where I had worked at Escapades.

He called fifteen minutes after midnight. My mother picked up the receiver.

"Who am I speaking to?" my mother asked, knowing full well to whom she was speaking.

"Sheldon? Your boyfriend is on the phone," my mother shouted, even though I was right beside her finishing the dessert component of my TV dinner.

I carried the phone as far away as the cord permitted, into the kitchen. Since my father had left, the decor in our house had undergone a transformation. Out went the Sears-Roebuck saloon doors that divided the kitchen from the TV room, up went the love beads.

Arnold told me he wished he could be with me tonight. He was stuck at a party, hiding in the coatroom. The hosts of the party were old friends of his—fellow travelers from back in the Red Scare days. The husband now owned a fur shop in Beverly Hills; the wife was a big supporter of Israel. He didn't mention if E and her husband were in attendance, or if his own wife, who must have been wondering where her husband had gone, was nearby.

He must have been wondering where my mother was. Phone cords in those days rarely reached past twelve feet.

I began to cry, but with restraint, so as not to alarm my mother, who was listening on the far side of the love beads. But a teenage girl who has been stood up on New Year's Eve by her steady can rarely maintain restraint.

His response to my hysterical tears was to break up with me. For my sake. He didn't want me to spend another New Year's Eve crying.

I cried harder.

Between sobs, I put it to him this way: Why wouldn't he just tell E and his wife that he had fallen in love with someone else? I did not say, *with another woman*. I did not yet think of myself as a woman.

I might not have thought of myself as the "other woman," but I suspect that was a choice on my part. I wasn't ready to give up the benefits of youth. I had only begun to appreciate the shifting power of a thirty-year age gap, how the king can abruptly become the queen's pawn. I gave him two weeks to break up with his wife and E—or else. Then I hung up on him and repeated my ultimatum to my mother. She looked both stunned and terrified.

"*Or else* what?" my mother asked.

———

This is how the memoir portrays this next period in our courtship:

Next day [New Year's Day], I went to his studio. He was sitting on his cot, elbow on knees, head in hands. He looked spent. He hadn't even bothered to change into his painting pants. They sat on a chair, stiff and dried out. The old layers of paint were so thickly caked on, the material held the shape of him, an effigy of air. I lay down beside him and mashed my brow against his thigh. He ran his hand over my face, nape, throat, breast.

"This is just as intolerable for me as it is for you," he said.

We took counsel and tried to figure out what we could do. It was apparent to both of us that our love wasn't going to end anytime soon. Around dusk, I grew despondent again and he tried to make light of things, but his hilarity sounded like a scream from a cage.

Two weeks later, he left his wife and we moved in together. When I told my mom, she got a migraine that lasted four days.

Whoa!

First, he had to break up with E.

According to him, E had known for some time that their relationship was over. She and her husband were trying yet again to save their marriage. She was taken aback that he had fallen in love so quickly but was happy for him. The breakup was bittersweet.

I will wager the breakup would have gone differently if he had mentioned my age.

Next, he had to find the right time to tell his wife.

The phone rang during breakfast the day my ultimatum expired. My mother answered.

"It's Sheldon," she said, holding onto the receiver a beat longer than necessary when I tried to grab it.

I moved to the far side of the love beads.

"I told her," he said. He sounded like he had been crying.

"What did she say?"

"She asked if I was in love with E."

"Did you tell her about me?"

"Not yet."

After I hung up, while I was still intoxicated from the accomplishment of having Arnold give up not one but two women for me, my mother swept aside the love beads.

"Is he getting a divorce?" she asked. "Is he going to marry you?"

I accused her of being pitifully conventional, but in truth, I had not thought further than having him all to myself. The state of wishing and wanting was the only state I knew.

7

WITH ARNOLD'S ENCOURAGEMENT, I ENTERED THERAPY AROUND
the same time he left his wife. The only therapy I could afford was the
free clinic, and the only spot available for someone my age was in a teen
group for recovering heroin addicts. The only other nonaddict in the
group was a nineteen-year-old girl who'd recently had sixteen feet of
her large intestine removed and now wore a colostomy bag for life. She
tried not to cry when we went around the circle and it was her turn to
name her biggest fear.

"That no one will ever love me wearing this bag of shit," she
whispered.

The therapist, a UCLA graduate student who was trying to rack
up clinical hours, held out his hand for us to examine. His pinky was
missing.

"Did a dog bite it off?" asked the boy with the week-old needle
marks.

"A saw?" ventured the girl who had tried to sell me her methadone
before group.

"It's the first thing people notice about me," the therapist told us.

I hadn't noticed the stump before, and from the expressions of the addicts, they hadn't either.

"Everyone, including me, has something missing. We can't let that determine our lives."

My biggest fear—when my turn came—was that I wasn't talented enough to get into art school. This hardly impressed the addicts. Though some of them had found God, they hadn't heard the commandment *Give me genius or give me death*. With Arnold's help, I had been working on my portfolio, a series of charcoal drawings of explicit sexual acts from the vantage point of the woman. In my artist statement, I proposed to turn these sketches into an animated short film.

I had been in group for about three weeks when Arnold called to tell me he'd left his wife. As I took my seat in the circle that afternoon, I must have looked more confused than exhilarated by his news because the therapist challenged me to open up to the group.

I had already told them that I was seeing a married man thirty years my senior. To an addict, not one of the boys or girls approved. Despite the messes they had made of their own adolescence, they believed that I had made an even worse choice. The girls in particular found the idea of having an old man kiss them icky.

"You're not creeped out when he touches you?"

"Does he get boners?"

"Are you ever worried he's going to have a heart attack or a stroke or something when he's balling you?"

I wasn't, until she said that.

I didn't yet know how to explain to the group that his age was my aphrodisiac, that I needed to be desired by someone older and important so that I could feel special. The fact that *he was old enough to be my father* was what elevated me above the line of wallflowers, girls who had to wait for boys their own age to ask them to dance.

And let us be frank: I didn't want to have to wait my turn in line with those girls for all the goodies adulthood was offering.

But that morning after he told me that he had left his wife and wanted us to live together, I realized that jumping my place in line had consequences. Did I really want to live with a middle-aged man? What if I changed my mind? I had only had sex with three boys before Arnold (the one to whom I lost my virginity, his best friend, and a guy I shared my mattress with at the squat on Avenue D). Doesn't becoming a great artist require a constant variety of new sexual partners? It did for all the male artists.

There are no doubts about my decision in the memoir. The May-December (or in my case April-December) aspect of our courtship is always portrayed as divine madness. Erotic love requires the bodies be present, yet the only description of what middle age had been up to with his body was the loose skin around his neck, and I remedied that by having him wear a T-shirt.

Where are the loving descriptions of his body, the object of my mad desire?

To have described his body in my memoir would have required that I look—really look—at his then seventy-five-year-old body and hurry to my computer to try to remember it in his youth, or our version of his youth, middle age.

"He left his wife today," I told the group.

"Is he going to move into your place?"

"I live at home with my mom. She wouldn't exactly appreciate that," I said.

———

Let us not forget my mother's migraine.

My mother was forty-one, but looked twenty-five, a blonde since sixteen. To supplement the $140 a month my father paid in child support, she worked as a saleswoman (strictly commission, wholesale) representing everything from Funkadelic jumpsuits to Afghan sheep coats (on rainy days my brothers and I would bag the coats lest they smell like wet sheep). After a long, dispiriting day, before she came home to feed us, she would meet up with one of her divorcée friends at the Fireside Inn, a cardinal-red singles' bar with free happy hour hors d'oeuvres. Until the year before, she had never had sex with anyone but my father, and he hated to touch and be touched. 1971 was the apogee of the carefree decade between the pill and AIDS. She slept with cowboys who wore dinner-plate-size silver belt buckles and salesmen whose last names she forgot to ask. She had cunnilingus performed on her for the first time. When the phone rang late one night, and heavy breathing answered her "Hello, hello," it took her a few minutes to realize that the breather wasn't a man she was dating but an obscene caller.

My mother's migraine had not abated when I got home from group that afternoon. She was in our bed with a pillow over her head to block sunlight and muffle sound. I heard her whimpering, but I wasn't sure if it was because of the headache—or me.

I started quietly packing my duffel bag, the same one I had packed for New York.

The pillow spoke. "Where are you going?"

She knew I was going to him, but she didn't know where that was. "He's staying at a friend's house in Bel Air."

I mentioned Bel Air because I thought it would impress my mother. She and I had toured the tony canyon after the last fire swept through to see which of the movie stars' homes had been leveled.

"Another man will be there?"

"I know what I'm doing," I said. "He loves me."

"I give up," the pillow said. "Maybe he'll tame you."

Interesting choice of words, *tame*. Did she mean domesticate, or train, or break, as in a young filly must be broken before she is ridden? My mother had read and believed every word of Betty Friedan's *The Feminine Mystique*. She had come out of her divorce certain that our poverty was her fault, but Betty had straightened her out. She had no credit because in 1971 credit cards and mortgages were issued only in the man's name. My mother had warned me never to become reliant on a man, never to allow myself to get trapped in marriage and have to chew off my own leg to escape, as she had.

8

Arnold and I rented a hillside bungalow, halfway between his studio and CalArts. The bungalow came with modular furniture and was cantilevered over a freeway. During morning rush hour, the kitchen floor shook, and the surface of our coffee pitched and sloshed. Sometimes, late at night, lying beside Arnold, the ceaseless whoosh of tires sounded like a wave that never reaches the shore.

THE READER SHOULD NOT NECESSARILY TRUST SETTING— place—in a memoir. Too often, it is distorted by nostalgia (the honey-colored meadow that is no more) or by trauma (the ominous shadow under the dank basement doorjamb).

But in describing our actual first place together—the Bel Air house, absent from the memoir—I am speaking about a different kind of setting: negative space. In a painting (as Arnold had taught me), negative space is the empty shapes between, within, and surrounding the subject matter—a king, a fruit bowl, a ballerina. In writing, negative space is silence, what is not said. Positive space may be the reason for the artwork's existence, but negative space is just as important. It shares edges with positive space. Its absence creates form, proportion, and dimensionality.

Now compare the description of our first place together from the memoir (what my middle-aged self had chosen as the positive space)—"a hillside bungalow"—with the actual setting.

———

The Bel Air house was where the New Year's Eve party had taken place only three weeks before. The furrier and his wife were off to winter in Israel, and Arnold was supposed to house-sit. The furrier had warned Arnold not to mention to his wife that I would be moving into the master suite with him. But at the last minute, their adult son and his girlfriend showed up and commandeered the suite for themselves. Arnold and I were relegated to the five-year-old granddaughter's room. The granddaughter—named Ninel, *Lenin* spelled backward—was traveling with her grandparents.

The bedroom walls were princess pink. The canopied bed was flounced in purple sequined gauze. The white shag carpet was ankle deep. Every drawer in the Queen Anne bureau was crowded with Barbies. There was so much doll hair, even with the drawers shut, tufts stuck out.

The irony of our landing in a pedophile's daydream was not lost on me. I found it funny, but it troubled him. He could not get an erection on the Barbie sheets. We bought neutral sheets. It didn't help. He said we needed to get out of there, but he had no money. He had given his wife the house, the bank accounts, the better car.

(If you leave your wife for another woman, you might horse-trade for the better car, but if you leave your wife for a teenager, you take only your toothbrush.)

———

A friend of his, an art collector, offered a loan—to be paid back in artwork—but only on the condition that he get to meet the teenager who had broken up a marriage. Arnold didn't say as much, but I sensed I was part of the transaction. The collector owned a steel plant, three homes, had grandchildren and a wife of forty years, and also a mistress not much older than me.

We met at the collector's version of Ah Fong's, a Japanese shabu-shabu restaurant with private rooms and servers who looked like geishas. He arrived with his mistress, who dressed her part—black dress, evening bag, heels, which she left by the shoji screen door. I wore bell-bottoms and gladiator sandals with tire-tread soles.

It was the first time I saw our age difference mirrored in another couple. The mistress had to help the collector sit on the tatami floor. When he took her hand, it looked like Father Time clasping onto a new branch. He was only five years older than Arnold.

A geisha brought us hot towels.

"Domo," the mistress said.

"She's taking Japanese classes," the art collector said.

After I washed my hands and face, I didn't know where to leave the wet cloth.

"The oshibori goes in the basket," the mistress said. "You weren't supposed to wash your face with it, just your hands." Her voice sounded kind, but her look said, *You're an amateur at this.* My return look said, *I'm not a gold digger like you because mine has no gold.*

"I hear you're applying to art school," the collector said.

I told him that I had just been accepted by CalArts (Disney's version of the Bauhaus) and now had to wait to hear if I got a scholarship.

The mistress smiled. The smile said, *Mine is paying for the Japanese classes* and *an apartment.*

When the dumplings arrived, I felt vindicated. I was able to use chopsticks and she needed a fork.

We did not exchange another word the entire dinner. While the men talked, we communicated by how subservient or dominant we behaved toward our elders. Shabu-shabu is a soup whose raw ingredients are served on separate trays—seafood, meats, vegetables, noodles, and eggs. The meal requires that someone on each side of the table take charge of the cooking.

She picked up a piece of fish (with a fork), held it under the boiling broth before serving it to the art collector.

I reached for a mushroom (with chopsticks), doused it, and then ate it myself.

She floated leaves of cabbage on the soup's roiling surface, then ladled them into the collector's bowl before serving herself.

I let Arnold cook for me.

About halfway through the meal, I began to understand her strategy. Arnold was serving me what he liked to eat, while she was eating just what she wanted; all she had to do was serve the collector first.

Her smile said it all.

When the collector couldn't eat another bite, she surprised me again. She lay back on the pillows and let him massage her feet. She did not close her eyes but watched me instead. I knew that if I stretched out, dropped my feet in Arnold's lap, he would massage my feet, too. Two Father Times massaging four young feet in a geisha establishment. It was too depressing to contemplate. I let my feet fall painfully asleep rather than give her the satisfaction we were alike.

After the check was paid (by the collector), she easily slipped on her heels while I had difficulty buckling my numb feet into my gladiator sandals.

9

MY MOTHER AND I HAD NOT SPOKEN SINCE SHE HAD HANDED MY reins to Arnold with the instructions "Tame her." But she broke the silence to relay a message from CalArts. An interview had been arranged with the dean of the film school, a British director of note whose movies—*The Ladykillers, The Man in the White Suit*—my mother and I had watched on *The Million Dollar Movie*. My scholarship depended on me impressing him, or at least that was how I saw it. I don't remember what I wore to the interview, so I will borrow a typical outfit from a photograph taken of me around the same time. I sport hip-hugger denim bell-bottoms with hems as wide as basketball hoops. My top is a tight, ribbed, short-sleeved T. I never wore a bra.

Between the dean's smoker's cough and his Scottish accent, I didn't understand a word he said. He invited a few faculty members into his office to meet me, all men, all bearded and dressed as if for a Be-In. I assumed their curiosity about me was an affirmation of my talent, not the fact that I had submitted the San Fernando Valley version of the *Kama Sutra*. I thought these men wanted to ask me about negative space.

"You're awfully young to take on this sort of project," said the head of animation, a comb-over in a Nehru jacket, as he leafed through my storyboards: missionary position, fellatio, cunnilingus, sixty-nine, standing up, doggie style. He put a fatherly hand on my shoulder. "I mean, the scope of your project. Do you understand how many cells you would need to draw for a thirty-minute film?"

"Just under eighteen thousand," I said.

"What made you decide on this subject matter?" asked the conceptual artist, infamous for his six-minute video about miniature toy cars and trucks driving out of his foreskin. He flanked my other side. My shoulder was already taken so he rested his hand on my back as he reached for my flip-book, titled "Doggie-style."

As he flipped through the pages, the dean remained in his chair, but the other faculty, a documentary filmmaker and an acting coach, pressed closer for a better look. The animated images were small and not easily identifiable. One sequence showed the wallpaper going in and out of focus; another had my breasts hanging down and jiggling with every thrust; a third caught a man's hand gripping my shoulder for stability and force.

"I thought it was about time," I said (I was still seventeen), "that sex be shown from the woman's point of view."

I got the scholarship!

Was our transaction that afternoon—a full scholarship in exchange for sexual arousal—even steven, or did these men take advantage of me? Or did I take advantage of them?

CalArts was one of those cutting-edge hubs that collected outrage like magnets amass iron shavings. The campus, a mammoth three-story edifice financed by Disney, already looked dated, as only futuristic designs can look dated, before the paint dried. Rumors circulated that Disney had built the campus to be converted into a hospital should the world ever tire of an avant-garde art college.

I enrolled in two electives and a critical thinking requirement,

Human Sexuality. The professor opened each class with a question: "What aroused you this week?" One by one, the gas station attendant's son, the nephew of the king of Thailand, the girl who had dropped acid before class would describe the texture of silk socks, a roommate's girlfriend's breasts, the sensation of a detachable showerhead against a clitoris. The professor would close each class by turning off the lights so we could masturbate (through our clothes, only ourselves) in the dark. If the professor, a psychologist who sometimes taught barefoot, gave lectures between the opening question and the closing exercise, I don't remember them.

My first elective was an easy choice, a conceptual art seminar. I gravitated to the cutting edge, and conceptual art had only edges, no positive or negative space, just the fissures in between. Unlike traditional painting and animation, conceptual art wasn't stuck in tired, problem-solving reality. Did I really need to draw all 18,000 cells for my movie when the concept—doggie style from a woman's point of view—was stronger *and* sexier than sitting through a thirty-minute animation of the wallpaper going in and out of focus?

The demographics of the students interested in conceptual art skewed male, and though that might have alarmed me, all the demographics in all the majors skewed male, except the feminist art program with its looms and consciousness-raising sessions.

I considered myself a feminist but not that kind of feminist. I didn't want to be a girl who threw her hat only into the ladies' ring. My ambition was to have my art immortalized one day on a slide in an art history lecture—even though it was evident from the artists listed on the syllabi that women need not apply. I was not going to let my sex stand in my way, as if femaleness were an obstacle or a hunter's blind.

Before rejecting the feminist art program, however, I did attend one consciousness-raising session. That afternoon, the first week of classes, the group had decided to look at their own wombs with the help of a speculum and a mirror. I had no desire to see my own cervix. The idea seemed distasteful to me in a way that group masturbation wasn't. But to decline would have made me seem less enlightened than these girls who had decided to forgo seeking men's approval.

Here was what I saw when my turn came and I looked in the mirror: pink, moist, healthy tissue with a tiny entrance into my womb, a womb that would never bear children and would one day turn cancerous. But that afternoon, it looked like the bodily equivalent of meaning.

There was a camaraderie among these women that didn't exist in the posed aloofness of the conceptual artists. I was lonely for female company. I missed my mother. Living with Arnold for the past four months had isolated me. Yet I never returned to have my consciousness raised. I didn't believe a group of women had the authority to pronounce me an artist.

I was about to register for my second elective when the acting coach—fortyish, blond Fabio hair—waved me over and suggested I take an independent study in acting techniques with him.

I was flattered that he remembered me. "When do we start?" I asked.

"Now?" he asked back.

As he led me to his office and closed the door behind us, he said, "You seem nervous."

"I've never taken an acting class before," I admitted.

"We're not going to act in this first session, we are just going to breathe."

"I already know how to do that," I said.

Was I flirting?

"By learning to breath in unison, I can show you, not just *tell* you, about exercises for inhabiting a character."

He turned off the light and we both sat cross-legged on the floor. The carpet was brand-new and still smelled of chemicals.

For what I thought was at least five minutes, but turned out to be less than one, I tried to imitate his breathing, which he varied as a tango dancer might abruptly change tempo.

He turned on the lights. "It's not working. You're not keeping up," he said.

I waited for instructions while he considered how to fix me.

"I'm going to take off my clothes," he said.

I tried to remember if he had locked the door after he shut it, not because I was worried that he would rape me but because I was embarrassed should someone walk in.

Peeling off his T and shimmying out of his jeans (he did not wear underwear), he said, "You don't have to undress *unless* you feel clothes are inhibiting your breathing." My hip-huggers cut into my hips as I sat cross-legged on the floor. My basket-weave leather belt dug into my flesh. I undressed. I believed I knew the difference between getting naked for art and modeling at Escapades.

He turned off the lights again, but I could still see him in the ambient light. He was sitting beside me, his penis semierect.

"It's normal, just ignore it," he said when he saw me looking at it.

We began breathing again, him instigating, me attempting to follow.

"You're so tense," he said. He reached over and massaged my shoulders.

I would be a liar to say it didn't feel good.

"Lie down," he said. "I'm going to give you a proper massage."

I lay prone while he straddled my thighs and started rubbing my back. He did not reach for my breasts or vagina, so I assumed the massage was legit. I could feel his erection growing firmer. A drop of precum stunned me with its liquid warmth. I flinched.

"It's not semen," he explained. "I have a kidney infection."

A second drop fell. A third.

I could have pushed him off, made a scene, reported him to the head of performance art, the conceptual artist who featured his fore-skin in a video. Or I could pretend that I wasn't prudish about having a stranger's erect penis drip semen or urine—it hardly mattered at that point—on me.

At least at Escapades, the men were not allowed to touch.

I dropped my independent study that afternoon and told no one at school why.

But I did tell Arnold.

"What do you mean he had you undress?"

"He was teaching me about synchronized breathing."

"Naked?"

"Clothes inhibit."

"That's why we wear them," he said.

In a derisive tone I had previously used only with my mother, I said, "I know what I'm doing."

———

There are two voices in every memoir: old and young. For the previous scene, I employed the young voice by doing one simple trick. I took reflection out of the equation. The young voice doesn't reflect; it just reacts.

Take these two sentences: "I had no desire to see my own cervix. The idea seemed distasteful to me in a way that group masturbation wasn't."

The old voice might have stopped the narrative to ask why group masturbation was more acceptable than womb gazing.

The old voice might have posited the answer: In 1971, what was sexually distasteful was adjudicated by men.

10

AT FIRST, I TOLD NO ONE AT CALARTS ABOUT MY "OLD MAN,"
slang for boyfriend in those days. The omission, I thought, was because
I wanted to be my own person, not some "old man's" girlfriend. But
now I suspect it was because I was ashamed of Arnold. I feared that if
my peers found out that I was in love with a middle-aged art teacher
who taught retirees and still believed in traditional painting, I might be
excluded from the "in" crowd, which consisted entirely of young men
who believed painting was dead.

Once the memoir reaches the CalArts years, I tell the reader almost
nothing more about Arnold. He makes a few more appearances in the
pages, has a few more lines of dialogue, but the story about the older
man preying on the underage girl is over.

I turned eighteen.

Half a Life is a bildungsroman, a story of education. *Bildungsroman* is
a more accurate term than *coming of age*. After all, one can come of age
and learn nothing.

A bildungsroman implies that the hero, after many missteps and
false starts, has finally found the key to unlock his or her true destiny.

For male narrators, the bildungsroman traditionally ends with the hero about to embark on his avocation, be it sexual conquests or working with lepers. For female protagonists, the bildungsroman classically ends in marriage.

(A Jane Austen heroine never wakes up years after the wedding to see that the pixie dust of white-hot love is now ashen gray hair, and the young man she married is now an aging animal in need of help.)

I stopped our story at the age of consent. My forty-five-year-old self believed that to continue our story into domesticity would have been at the expense of my own narrative trajectory. I did not want to write about a middle-aged man who had given up his kids and house and car and bank accounts for a teenager.

A story stops when the writer doesn't know what to say next; it ends when there is nothing more to be said.

II

Over the next four years, every weekday morning, Arnold went to his studio while I drove to CalArts on the concrete overpasses that traversed the valley.

THIS IS ONE OF THE LAST MENTIONS OF ARNOLD IN THE MEMoir's pages. The declarative statement implies that we both set out every day with purpose and work. What I did not mention was that his studio, what had looked to me, at sixteen, like a laboratory of experimentation, looked to him, at forty-seven, like a diorama of failure.

He had once been part of a cadre of social realists smelted by the Great Depression and forged during the Second World War, men who believed that art shouldn't only gratify the elite but be comprehensible to the masses. There were no women social realists, none at least who rated a slide in an art history lecture.

He had been raised in a sprawling immigrant Jewish clan outside Buffalo, New York. His father and mother, unable to assimilate, had remained embedded in the family, working for more ambitious siblings who owned sewing shops and clothing stores.

Arnold turned seven at the start of the Great Depression. When his uncles could no longer afford to support their brother, his father went to work for a jeweler. Ten hours a day, in tenements and alleyways right out of an Ashcan School painting, he knocked on doors offering to buy gold jewelry and keepsakes from suspicious but desperate residents. At eight years old, Arnold watched an old couple pull out their gold molars with a pair of pliers, wash off the blood, and give them to his father. His father then weighed the couple's teeth on a hand scale (supplied by the jeweler). Arnold described the couple's diminishing hope as his father removed one counterweight (0.01 ounces) after another to even out the balance. The weight of the teeth yielded less than a dollar.

His family was religious enough to see that he was bar mitzvahed, but not religious enough to make him attend shul after that.

He attended a public all-boys technical high school to study advertising design and sign painting. Dreaming about becoming a fine artist during the grim decade was as ludicrous as him believing he would one day be king.

He dated girls his own age, necked with them on Buffalo's only beach, a rim of sand on the Canadian side of Lake Erie. On the ferry ride home one Sunday, he met his first wife. He liked her well enough, but he wanted to go to ArtCenter School of Design in Los Angeles, become an adman. He didn't want to waste his life painting *Going Out of Business* signs in Buffalo, the only signs around in 1939.

Everyone suspected another war was fermenting. His parents stopped hearing from their cousins in Germany. Their letters were stamped *Rückkehr* (return). No forwarding address.

He was working nights at a factory, saving for school, when Pearl Harbor was bombed. Rather than wait to be drafted, he and some buddies enlisted in the signal corps, figuring the war might be over by the time they learned the math. At the physical, because of migraines, his draft card was magically stamped *4F*.

A month later, he was on the train for Los Angeles, his girlfriend forgotten. He was the only young man in his car not in uniform. He hinted he was a spy. Los Angeles was seventy-nine degrees when he stepped off the train that January 1943. The winter sun was powerful enough to make wearing sunglasses stylish. The future adwomen in his classes dressed in sleeveless blouses and capris. This was the first time in the school's history that women outnumbered men, but enrollment was needed. While the men had been slogging through Europe and New Guinea, a new industry had been born: television.

These future adwomen behaved differently than the girls he had dated in Buffalo. With their ponytails and athletic postures, they possessed a wry confidence that his Buffalo girlfriend, the daughter of a ragman, lacked.

He was twenty-one. He had only had sex with his girlfriend, who in her inexperience believed him to be experienced. The future adwomen would know how unskilled he was before he got their brassieres unclasped. Despite his sunglasses and fashionably patched jeans (*WEAR IT OUT—MAKE IT DO. Our labor and goods are fighting for you!*), he was lonely. He sent for his girlfriend, but not before marrying her.

He should have waited another semester before summoning her. He realized that only after she had quit her job as a salesgirl, packed her two suitcases' worth of belongings, slammed the door on her ragpicker father, and moved across the country into his tiny studio apartment at the foot of the Hollywood Hills. The glamour of spotlights sweeping the night sky to announce movie premieres made her feel as if she had just fallen off a turnip truck.

She had never heard of television, and no matter how many times he explained its workings, she didn't understand how a moving picture could be seen without a projector.

He began to make new friends and she just didn't fit in. She was both too serious, and not serious enough. His crowd, mostly women and a few lucky fellows with 4Fs, grew up around the movie business. They spoke about the war in a way that upset her. Her war began with the Nazis rounding up the Jews. Their war had begun in Spain six years earlier, after Franco encouraged German war planes to incinerate the town of Guernica and the West did nothing to retaliate. They rallied enthusiastically in favor of a Soviet-American war effort.

A few in his crowd were already Party members. (He would later carry his own wallet-size card with *Communist Party of America: Hollywood Chapter* stamped under his picture.) He started reading Marx while his wife leafed through movie magazines. After a CP meeting one night (his wife never wanted to go), he had sex with a comrade in her car. He had found his confidence in the intoxicating confluence of politics and sex.

Truman dropped two atomic bombs on Japan, and the emperor finally surrendered. As jubilation and hurrahs filled the streets, his crowd asked, Was the second bomb necessary?

He got a job at Warner Bros., as an assistant art director, drawing storyboards for a Tarzan movie, *King of the Jungle* (a bildungsroman, by the way). Hollywood went on strike a week later, October 5, 1945. The picket line was walked by movie stars and screenwriters and artists—not commercial admen who sucked on capitalism's tit, but WPA muralists who painted sets by day and studied the Mexican muralists by night. He was invited to go landscape painting with them. He taught himself to paint by imitating their brushstrokes.

He left his wife with their one-year-old son (the daughter my age hadn't been born) and traveled to Mexico to study at the source, with Rivera and Siqueiros.

He realized he would need more life drawing if he were to paint with any kind of acumen and abandon. He was twenty-eight already. By twenty-eight, Picasso had already finished his Rose and Blue Periods. Arnold had the same artistic aspirations that I would one day have, to get his own slide in an art history carousel, or his version of that ambition—the technology of the slide carousel had not yet been invented.

Every afternoon, a different young woman came to his studio, a narrow storefront on Fairfax, and undressed for him. Twisted in a chair or sprawled across the model stand, some had breasts that defied gravity; others had breasts that changed shape with every new position. Nipples came in different forms—inverted, flat, protruding. Areolas ranged in color from burnt sienna to magenta. Some pubic mounds were forested; others only had grass along the banks. The drawings only excelled if he and the model experienced a connection, a compulsion to render and a need to be seen.

To supplement his income, he drove a lunch truck through San Pedro's wharves and factory district. He drew longshoremen, painted workers in slaughterhouses, workers playing craps on lunch breaks (the Party chastised him for showing workers in a bad light).

He knew he was being tailed by the FBI. Everyone in his crowd was. What he did not know was which of the models he was sleeping with would turn out to be an informant. The FBI paid twenty-five dollars for a tip. He only paid ten dollars for a three-hour modeling session.

(Forty years later, he would read the heavily redacted 760-page dossier the FBI had kept on him and try to figure out if the redhead with whom he'd thought he was in love, and on whom he finally mastered cunnilingus, had ratted him out.)

He had a solo exhibit at the Pasadena Museum of Art. He won first prize in a juried exhibition at the Los Angeles County Museum of Art (a painting of Julius and Ethel Rosenberg's last kiss before their executions) the same year—1958—that I won first place in my elementary school for my crayon drawing of a rearing horse.

He began what he believed were his most important paintings to date, the War Series, inspired by the photographs of the concentration camp survivors taken only minutes after they had been liberated. When he first showed his father the photographs in *LIFE* magazine just after the war, his father spent hours with a magnifying glass looking for his cousins among the living skeletons. Arnold painted eighteen canvases—*Celebration of the Survivors, The Raped, The Phoenix Bird, Dance of the Survivors, The Survivors, The Death Cart,* to name a few. He painted and drew with a superhuman intensity that artists feel only once or twice in a life, the galloping exhilaration when a story reveals itself faster than you can get it down.

The War Series was exhibited to some fanfare in the inaugural show of a gallery downtown. The press was excellent, a rave in the *Los Angeles Times,* but nothing sold. Who wants concentration camp survivors, even those dancing in celebration of their freedom, on their living room walls?

He opened a school with a few other struggling social realists and started spending more time teaching than in his studio.

The late '50s were America's economic boom years. The Red Scare had all but saturated Hollywood. The stars and screenwriters and art directors who had once bought his art were blacklisted. The polemics of social realism were not only out of fashion; they were dangerous. Abstract painting was in. Art was no longer about stirring the masses, but about interiority and process.

He tried his hand at abstraction, but it was lonely in his studio without the models. He found that pushing paint around without the goal of creating imagery felt pointless. He couldn't let go of the belief that art had something to teach—empathy, humility; otherwise it was only decoration. The more he faltered as an artist, the more he chased women.

He had a constant supply now in his private classes, wives whose husbands played golf or traveled for work or were dead. Someone always wanted to be the teacher's pet. And the models. They now posed for his students (he had stopped painting), but that only made the assignations in his private studio next door sexier.

The models stayed the same age as he grew older. He put on weight for the first time. Two gray streaks, one under each nostril, appeared in his beard. He let his hair grow long, not hippie long, but artist length.

He called women "love" and "sweetheart" so he would not mix up their names. He thought he was in love with a twenty-four-year-old redhead. He had an affair with a director friend's twenty-year-old stepdaughter. By the time he looked up from his private orgy, abstraction was out. Pop art was in.

He was forty-five, disgusted with himself for having wasted a decade. He settled down to one wife and one mistress (age appropriate) and entered psychoanalysis.

The drawings of his that I had seen at his wife's gallery (the dancing Holocaust survivors that had electrified me with the gusto of his charcoal strokes applied to such fragile beings) had been done ten years before.

12

MY "OLD MAN" DID NOT REMAIN A SECRET AT SCHOOL FOR LONG. Arnold knew the dean of the art department, a second-generation abstract expressionist who had refused to include ceramics in the curriculum because "we are not the Hopi Indians." They had met years before when they had shared a wall in a group exhibition. Arnold had once loaned the dean keys to his studio for a tryst.

On our cot?

Early in my first semester, the two men met for lunch and Arnold confessed to the dean that he had fallen in love with me. I worked in the art office as part of my scholarship, so the dean knew me by name. The dean wanted to wager Arnold a hundred dollars that our relationship would not last the year. When Arnold didn't bite, the dean sweetened the ante—would not last six months.

"Did you take the bet?" I asked.

"He is just jealous," Arnold said.

The dean ruled over about twenty faculty. Except for the feminist art program, all were men. As the scuttlebutt that I lived with a man their age circulated among them, I sensed a subtle—and not so subtle—

change in the way they interacted with me. The assistant dean started stopping by my desk in the art office to rub my shoulders while I typed rejection letters to artists who had applied for teaching positions. My task was to type the name of the artist next to the salutation so that the recipient did not notice it was a form rejection. When I complained that his massage was causing me to make typos, he said, "These are artists no one ever heard of." One day Arnold's name appeared on the list of rejected applicants. I must have been momentarily enraged at his intrusion into my world before another, more pervasive emotion took over. It wasn't pity, though it resembled pity. It wasn't sympathy, because sympathy was too saccharine, and this emotion had no consoling sweetness. It wasn't empathy, because I could not imagine what it was like to be middle-aged and rejected for a job with a form letter. What I felt was closer to love, but without the nagging dreaminess. This emotion was all about clarity.

I read the rejection form that I had been sending out blindly. It was surprisingly encouraging. The letter said that there was no job at present and wished the applicant luck securing a position elsewhere. The dean's signature looked real. It wasn't that much of a stretch to think the dean wrote it personally.

I rolled the form letter into my typewriter's carriage and adjusted the paper guides. I typed *A* after *Dear,* then leaned in to inspect the lineup. It was off. I tore out the letter, and then inserted another until I got one right. I would make sure that he never learned that he had not even rated a personal rejection from the dean.

My second act of compassion was to never tell him that it had been I who had typed the letter. It finally sank in: To love wasn't just to feel love, but to act lovingly.

At about the same time, Arnold had begun to paint again. The results were shaky and uneven. I knew he wanted my approval of his nascent attempts, and the reversal of power was both intoxicating (the manic euphoria of being eighteen years old and full of opinions) and distressing (I no longer believed that painting was relevant).

How a piece of art is judged has always been unstable. In the Middle Ages, for instance, a painting was either deemed good, in the service of God, or evil, in the service of the devil. At the height of the Romantic period, say, the 1700s in England, a painting was either pronounced beautiful, a Platonic idealization of nature, or ugly, showing nature unadorned, full of thorns and serpents. In 1971 at CalArts, a piece of art was either redrawing the boundaries of art—or it was pointless.

One day, as I opened his studio door to pronounce judgment, I smelled varnish. The scent heralded completion. In the many times I had visited the studio, he had never before felt his efforts were worthy of protecting.

There was a small canvas on the wall, an unimposing size, maybe a square foot. I was the subject matter. He had rendered me naked, in profile, sitting on the edge of our bed, looking over my shoulder at the observer. I had never before seen myself from his point of view.

The girl in the painting wasn't a nymph or a victim or a survivor or a sugar baby or a gold digger or a bimbo or a fatherless girl desperately in need of an older man's affection. The girl in the painting had a steely confidence in the knowledge that she was loved.

I had never seen that girl before.

I had seen someone who looked like her in the mirror, but whenever I caught my reflection, I became stiff and my expression turned artificial.

There was nothing artificial about this girl. This girl was loved, and she knew it. But her radiance came from another light source: This girl knew how to love back.

He showed me who I might become.

In the Greek myth, Pygmalion, a sculptor fed up with women in general, carves his ideal woman out of ivory and then falls in love with the beauty of his creation. He prays to the gods to metamorphose the inanimate ivory into living flesh so that he might be loved in return. The gods allow him to administer the breath of life with a kiss, and Pygmalion and his statue go on to be married. She bears him a daughter and a son. As time passes, her ivory face ages, her ideal breasts sag, her sculpted midriff grows stout, yet Pygmalion continues to love her.

I had sculpted my own version of the ideal man (gray temples, beard, my archetype fantasy of an artist), and he was turning into a human being in front of me.

13

MICHELLE HAD HER FATHER'S FEATURES—THE TRIANGULAR JAW, the animated eyebrows. I saw what Arnold must have looked like at our age, eighteen. I had become so intimate with his features over the past ten months, her face looked familial.

Was I her stepmother? Or were we supposed to become friends? She stood on our welcome mat, holding two bags of groceries. She wore a high-throated ankle-length "granny" dress, a throwback to pioneer life, popular in my old high school with girls who wore patchouli and believed in crystals.

Arnold hugged her for a long beat, then introduced us. We hesitantly smiled and shook hands. We did not meet each other's gaze. Our eyes were opposing magnets. Arnold had been answering all Michelle's questions about me during their weekly father-daughter dinners, but she had not yet asked my age, nor had he volunteered it. All she knew from her mother was that he had left *them* for a younger woman.

The week before, she had announced to Arnold that she was finally ready to meet me. Her therapist, a protégé of R. D. Laing who accepted Arnold's paintings as payment, agreed it was time. Under his guidance,

Michelle had selected an activity to do during her visit to relieve the stress of meeting me. She had chosen to cook a meal for her father.

As she followed Arnold into the kitchen, she took in the love nest her father had chosen over the family home. Our only furniture were two beanbag chairs, a mattress on the bedroom floor, and a card table with four folding chairs in the dining room. Our view was the Hollywood Freeway and a slice of the valley beyond. The sun had set behind the mountains, though it was only five o'clock. The valley was already in shadow. As Michelle looked out our windows, the lights of North Hollywood flickered on, one of which belonged to her mother.

Michelle still lived at home in her childhood bedroom. Was she there the night Arnold told her mother that he loved me and asked for a divorce? If Michelle had been home, she must have heard them arguing. If she hadn't been, she must have returned later that night to find her mother weeping, or raging, or both.

Did her mother conscript her into doing the detective work necessary to learn who I was? Her mother knew my name. She had demanded it the night Arnold left, but even so, what would my name tell her? I wasn't listed in the telephone book: The number was under my mother's name. Arnold's son, who was backpacking in Europe, had transferred to my high school for his senior year (the same graduating class as my older brother), so my picture was in his yearbook. But Michelle's mother never thought to look for her rival in her son's high school yearbook, among the freshmen, mind you.

As Arnold unpacked the groceries—three cans of tomato sauce, a brick of store-wrapped ground meat, and a box of spaghetti—Michelle continued her unguided tour of our house. She opened the first door she came to, a closet with my Sherpa coat and Arnold's bomber jacket sharing a hook. She opened the next door, the only bathroom. Earlier that day, I had removed my toiletries from view. I wasn't hiding that I lived there; I just didn't want her to know the details of how I attended to my body, which deodorant I used, what brand of tampon.

Arnold's first priority after we moved in had been to convert our second bedroom into my studio. We had pulled up the carpet and tacked museum board on the walls. As Michelle opened that door, she saw photographs of my latest performance piece lining the walls. The photographs chronicled me attempting to talk ants out of working, but if you didn't know the concept behind the imagery, it looked as if I were squatting over an anthill and talking to myself. Michelle wasn't looking at the photographs. All she saw was a second bedroom.

"Can I spend the night, Dad?"

Dread overcame me. "We don't have an extra bed," I said.

"We'll have one soon," Arnold promised. "You could always sleep on one of the beanbag chairs, but you'll probably wake up on the floor."

She found this riotously funny. Her laughter was like a runaway horse. Arnold bolted into laughter, too, but his laughter was like the rider who gallops alongside the frantic animal and tries to catch the loose reins.

He finally brought her to a halt by asking when dinner would be served.

She began frying the brick of meat. The pan she had chosen was too small and clumps of ground round landed on the stove top each time she stirred. Her laughter erupted again, but this time, Arnold remained silent.

I could sense her mood darken. By the time the noodles were drained, she had not spoken again, except to ask where we kept this spice and that utensil.

At our card table, Arnold and I sat across from each other, Michelle was in the middle.

He tasted her sauce and pronounced it delicious. He asked her how her Early Childhood Development class was going. When she told him she had dropped it, he encouraged her to try again. I thought he was being too solicitous until I realized it was not deference I was witnessing but fear. I couldn't tell if his fear was *of* his daughter or *for* her.

They ate with the same ebullient relish. Only after Arnold finished his second helping did she turn to me.

"What do you study at CalArts?" she asked.

"Conceptual art."

"What year are you in?"

I glanced over at Arnold. He looked stricken.

"We don't have *years* at CalArts," I said. "Only isms."

"What high school did you go to?"

I told her.

"My brother transferred there. Do you know Steven? Is that your car in the driveway? Do you like Judy Collins or Joan Baez better? Do you believe in ESP? Have you ever been in therapy? What were you doing in those pictures?"

She had noticed the photographs in my studio after all.

"I was trying to talk ants out of working," I said.

She doubled over, clutched her ribs, stamped her foot, her hilarity indistinguishable from hysteria. This time Arnold let her tire herself out. After dinner, she gave him the receipt for the groceries, and he reimbursed her, adding another twenty for fun money. I earned $1.60 an hour as a work-study student. I would have to type thirteen hours for that amount.

He drove Michelle home while I cleaned up. She had managed to land spaghetti sauce on the wall behind the stove. As I wiped it up, her laughter haunted me, but it hadn't sounded mocking, as if she left me to clean up her mess. It had sounded bewildered and hurt, as if her father had left her to clean up his mess.

———

"You saw for yourself," Arnold said, sitting on the edge of our mattress later that night. Hoarse with anguish, he confided to me a story he had never told anyone, even her mother, especially her mother. When the natal unit nurse brought Michelle, only a day old, to the hospital room for her feeding, the nurse practically shoved Michelle into his arms and said, "You take her."

He covered his face. His shoulders heaved. The only adult I had ever seen cry was my mother.

Was he crying for his daughter? Was I her replacement? Was this our commonality?

"I don't know how to help her," he said.

He remembered the first time he and his wife realized something was not right—she wasn't reaching the developmental milestones outlined in Dr. Spock's *The Common Sense Book of Baby and Child Care*. Between three and five, children were supposed to be able to distinguish between fantasy and reality. By age seven, children should be able to understand that their personal thoughts do not have a direct effect on the material world. Michelle missed those markers. She couldn't distinguish between her memories and make-believe. She remained in character—a princess, a witch—long after playtime was over, after her brother had shut himself into his room to get away from her. His wife stubbornly hoped that Michelle's eccentricities only indicated a high level of creativity, but Arnold suspected otherwise. Creativity requires an unflinching gaze on reality. Michelle couldn't focus. They saw specialists. She had every test. She couldn't correctly place the numbers on a clock face. Her pencil point couldn't find its way out of a maze. She was diagnosed with learning disabilities, borderline personality disorder, schizotypal personality disorder. She only learned to read because of her mother's patient determination. Did he tell me what a beautiful singing voice Michelle has? She could remember hundreds of tunes, thousands of lyrics. When she was sixteen, he found her pirouetting naked in the middle of the cul-de-sac. She told him she was Juliet (she had seen the Franco Zeffirelli film). She seemed to get better in the special high school they found for her. Then some jackass—Arnold wished he knew who—gave her LSD. It had taken a lot of therapy and time, but she had finally stabilized again and was—had been—taking a course at community college.

"I don't know how she'll react when she finally learns your age," he said.

"Why don't we tell her I'm twenty-one," I said.

"You sure?"

I didn't doubt that I could pull it off. I was happy to sacrifice a couple of years.

———

The second time I met Arnold's wife was shortly after Michelle's visit. The first time had been at her gallery when I was sixteen. Now she stood before me at the intake desk of a private psychiatric hospital in Burbank. Two nights before, Michelle had tried to set fire to the curtain in her bedroom. I was there to deliver a check for Arnold's half of the intake payment. Arnold was back East. His widowed mother, nearly ninety, was in the hospital in Buffalo.

Arnold's wife didn't know what I looked like, though by now various mutual friends of theirs who had met me must have described me to her. Wouldn't she have asked what I looked like? Or, perhaps, when your rival is eighteen, the specifics—hair color, eye color, height, weight, breast size—hardly matter.

She didn't appear to recognize me, and then she did.

The recognition was visceral. Every cord in her neck tightened. She jerked back from me as if I were a snake. Her eyes, Slavic and red-rimmed from having cried all night about her daughter, filled with rage and resignation. She waited a beat to see if I would acknowledge what I had done to her if only by returning her stare.

I did not return her stare, but I recognized it. My mother and her divorcée friends shared that same taut neck—the cables of fury—whenever they discussed their cheating exes. "After so many years, it's not losing the man that matters," they had all agreed, "it's losing the life." I had taken another woman's life and I knew it.

14

MY MOTHER WAS THE PERSON WITH WHOM I WOULD HAVE DIS-
cussed Michelle's disconcerting and mystifying behavior, but we were
not on speaking terms. Until she accepted my right to love whom I
pleased, I had nothing to say to her.

Around the same time that Michelle asked to meet me, my mother
finally agreed to meet Arnold. She only agreed because it did not look
as if I would talk to her otherwise. My brother Jack, two years my
senior, had warned me that our mother still fumed, wept, and specu-
lated whether or not Arnold was a pervert.

The pervading ethos gave her no clues. Was Chuck Berry a pervert
for taking a fourteen-year-old lover? Jerry Lee Lewis? Mick Jagger?
Wasn't groupie culture just statutory rape? And what about Gandhi,
who replaced his walking stick with two teenage girls he could lean on
by day and sleep naked beside at night? She told Jack that when she
was nineteen, back in Montreal, she had worked for a dashing forty-
something boss. He was married, but they flirted shamelessly. They
even necked once after an office party. But she was nineteen, not seventeen, and her boss didn't leave his wife for her.

In the end, I won the silence standoff. Arnold was invited to a family brunch.

———

Cosmopolitan magazine (circa 1970s) recommends five things a man should do the first time he meets his mother-in-law-to-be:

1. Don't show up empty-handed. Bring flowers, dessert, a bottle of wine, or a book about something that interests her.
2. Flatter her good taste. Gush over her latest watercolor or decorating scheme.
3. Take an interest in the family. Ask little brother what his favorite sports team is.
4. Offer to help out. Set the table or wash the dishes.
5. Talk about how grown up her daughter is, but don't kiss her daughter in front of her.

———

My mother and brothers still lived in the house my father had been banished from three years before, a new build at the foot of an unstable hill in Encino. A *For Sale by Owner* sign had been staked in the front yard for over a year. Our development had been carved out of landfill. Each rainy season, mud buried our backyard. In the dry season, refuse from the landfill—a lady's shoe, a hunk of rebar—would work its way out of the hardened mud, like a splinter out of skin. The neighbor's dog chewed off the sprinkler heads my father had installed himself. No one knew how to turn off the irrigation system, and no one wanted to call my father to ask. Geysers appeared at unexpected hours.

My older brother, Jack, a wry, scholarly boy with a Fu Manchu mustache, answered the door and was the first to shake Arnold's hand.

"I thought you'd be taller," Jack said.

My mother stood behind him waiting for me to introduce her. She wore tan corduroy bell-bottoms and wedge sandals. She was six years younger than Arnold, a bottle blonde, lithe, sexy, outgoing, fast with a quip, and fearsome when it came to her children. The last time she and Arnold had spoken was by phone, and Arnold was still going by the alias Sheldon.

"Gloria, Arnold." I had never before called my mother by her first name, and she looked surprised. Behind her, my two younger brothers—Tom, thirteen, and Pete, seven—took in the man my mother called "the perv."

Arnold had come empty-handed, in violation of *Cosmopolitan*'s number one rule. We had stopped by the supermarket earlier but couldn't decide on a gift. A bottle of wine seemed inappropriate because I was too young to drink. I nixed flowers and chocolates because I knew the expression of incredulity my mother's face would assume when she received the offerings.

My mother had set out a tray of cold cuts on the dining room table, her go-to buffet for family gatherings. Only a thin film of cellophane prevented my brothers from pouncing on the meat.

"It's so good to finally meet you, Gloria," Arnold said.

"Don't touch the meat!" my mother yelled over her shoulder at her sons.

Arnold walked into the living room, ankle deep in shag carpet. The house's foundation had shifted during the 1971 San Fernando earthquake, and the floors listed starboard. Love beads created room divisions. A rattan peacock chair flounced by an orange pom-pom pillow sat against the far wall. Framed posters of paintings my mother admired—Gauguin's *Are You Jealous?* and Orozco's *Revolutionaries Marching*—were hung salon style. But the coveted spot over the gas fireplace was reserved for my juvenilia.

As Arnold approached my portrait of an elderly Navajo woman whose likeness I had seen in *National Geographic,* I watched my mother's countenance waffle between deference and wrath. She wanted

Arnold to assure her that her daughter's talent was exceptional, that I had a future, while at the same time, she wanted to accuse him of stealing my future.

I had signed the painting with the pompous flair of a sixteen-year-old and dated my creation August 14, 1969, five months before I had started studying with him.

"No one had to teach her how to draw," Arnold said.

"I wish she still drew instead of talking to ants," my mother said.

"Were there any artists in your family, Gloria?"

My mother couldn't think of one.

"I like your taste," he said, admiring the Orozco. "Diego Rivera gets all the credit for the Mexican muralists, but Orozco was the better artist. Did you know he only had one arm?"

My mother didn't know.

"He was mixing explosives for fireworks and accidently blew off his left hand. He was fifteen, sixteen at the time. It probably saved his life. He had been planning to join Zapata and his revolutionaries and now he could only paint them instead."

He turned his attention to the Gauguin, two naked Tahitian girls, one seated, one supine, in a paradisiacal setting. "I've never understood the title, *Are You Jealous?* Do you?"

My mother hadn't known the painting had a title. She had chosen it for the colors.

"There doesn't appear to be any rivalry between the two women," Arnold said. He pointed to the seated figure. "Her likeness was borrowed from a kneeling figure on a frieze in Athens."

"How do you know?"

"Gauguin had a photograph of the frieze with him in Tahiti."

My mother had no higher education other than a six-week secretarial course. Her immigrant family had dismissed art as *treyf,* food for the goyim. As a girl, she had taken the streetcar to the art museum to see for herself and returned enough times to be able to say she had favorites.

"Maybe the jealousy wasn't between the two women," my mother said.

"Who then?"

"The artist and one of his models. Or both," she said.

After brunch, a jackal-pack eating frenzy around the tray of meat, Arnold asked Jack what his plans were after college.

"Medical school."

A few more pointed questions revealed Jack's biggest stumbling block in submitting his application, letters of recommendation. His UCLA premed courses had over a hundred students. He didn't know if any of the professors remembered him, let alone would speak up on his behalf. Most applicants had a family doctor to write them a reference, but we didn't have one. Our family doctor was the emergency room.

"One of my students is an ear, nose, and throat man. Talentless but a nice guy," Arnold said. "I think he graduated from UCLA. You should meet with him in person, explain your situation."

"Why would he do that for a complete stranger?" Jack said.

"Stop being so stubborn," my mother said to Jack. "Meet with the doctor."

"Do you want to meet my bird?" Pete asked. He returned from his bedroom with a blue parakeet dancing on his shoulder. My mother had clipped the bird's wings herself, and cut her youngest son's hair herself, and the jagged feathers and the jagged bangs matched.

"What's his name?" Arnold asked Pete.

"Her name," Pete corrected him. "Gloria."

Arnold laughed.

Pete was beside himself that Arnold understood that his naming the parakeet after our mother was supposed to be funny. He scooped up

Gloria and set her on Arnold's shoulder. The bird nibbled on Arnold's glasses, then hopped back to Pete's finger. Pete was now nestled beside Arnold on the couch.

"Want to hear her talk?" Pete asked Arnold.

"What does she say?"

" 'Gloria wants a cracker.' "

———

My mother had given up selling elephant-ear-collared disco shirts and now worked long hours at a figure salon, a prototype of a gym where women jiggled away fat with vibrating hip belts and beauty rollers. Tom was supposed to babysit Pete after school, but having recently reached puberty, Tom preferred to go through his metamorphosis in the privacy of his own room, locked from the inside. With no one to talk to, Pete would wander over to the construction site next door, earning candy money by picking up fallen nails for the crew. Like his sister before him, he gravitated to any man who paid attention to him. The foreman referred to him as "son" and showed him how to rub two nails together to create a magnet. One of the cabinet men laughed at his knock-knock jokes. The man at the pet store let him feed the birds.

I wince as I write the above paragraph: It should have been so obvious that something bad was going to happen to my little brother.

———

He was a neighbor with children of his own: a boy, thirteen, and a girl, ten. The boy was Tom's new friend. My mother had finally sold the Encino house for a song and moved with my two younger brothers to a beach town seventy miles south. She had driven there on a lark one sunny afternoon and found an Eden where her unsupervised sons could play on the beach until she came home. The move would require flexibility and coordination—she could only afford the rent offseason, but luckily, offseason coincided with the school year. Summers, they would need to pack up and move inland to a weekly-rental apartment. She had described for me the idyllic elementary school right on the beach that Pete would be attending. Recess was on the sand. And the middle school that Tom would go to sat on a bluff with views of the ocean. Her only worry was uprooting the boys twice a year, but now Tom, a solemn, private boy, had found a friend, Lance (I am not using his real name), who, like himself, was obsessed by cartography. When Tom asked if he could sleep over at Lance's house, my mother did due diligence: She called the boy's parents.

Later, she would remember asking the man who answered if his wife would be home, and then listening to a convoluted story about divorce and custody that struck her as more tiresome than suspicious, yet she caught a whiff of something that alarmed her, like the scent of a nearby fire. A moment later, the air smelled clear again, and she assumed she only imagined it.

When she dropped off Tom at his friend's house later that day, she had to admit that the house looked a lot nicer than the one she was renting, and the man, late forties, a Princeton cut right out of a barbershop poster, too middle management to be attractive to my mother (she was always looking), came out to her car and invited her in for coffee, which she declined because she had left Pete alone in the apartment. "Bring him next time," the man had said. "He can play with my daughter."

Tom and Pete shared a bedroom, so sleepovers were no fun at my mother's place. Tom and his friend had invented an urgent, all-consuming game that required Lance's model airplane collection. Tom pleaded to be allowed to spend the weekend. My mother worked Saturdays and needed Tom to look after Pete. She considered taking Pete with her, but last time he had come to the salon, he disappeared while she was measuring a customer's thighs and ended up being returned by the shopping mall's security guard. She didn't yet have any friends nearby with whom she could leave him.

She called Burt (I am using his real name) to explain the situation and ask if his offer for Pete to have a playdate with his daughter still stood. She promised to pick Pete up after work, around ten thirty.

He was welcome to spend the night, Burt told her. There was a bunk bed in his daughter's room. She could pick up both boys on Sunday.

A night to herself was awfully tempting. Besides, Tom would be in the next room.

Pete came home enchanted with the electric race car set that Burt had helped him assemble in the living room after his daughter fell asleep. It struck my mother as queer that a grown man would spend Saturday night entertaining his son's friend's little brother, unless the man was after the boy's mother.

Burt phoned a week later. He was taking his kids to Disneyland that Sunday and asked if Tom and Pete could join them. My mother waited a beat for Burt to ask her as well, but he misconstrued her hesitation and promised not to let Pete, who had a tendency to wander off, out of his sight. To allow her seven-year-old to go to Disneyland with a man she had only met for a second in a driveway seemed irresponsible, but to deny Pete a chance to go to Disneyland seemed heartless. She made Tom promise not to let Pete out of his sight.

Pete didn't stop talking about his adventures in Tomorrowland and how Burt had promised to take Tom and him camping soon.

The invitation came two weeks later: an overnight trip to Joshua Tree National Park. Burt owned two tents, one for himself and one for the kids. The wholesomeness of his enticements—a fantasy park, a nature adventure—caused my mother pause. Is a trip to Disneyland just another version of *I have candy in my car*?

My mother queried Tom, "Burt is never alone with Pete, is he?"

"It's unfair that I have to take Pete with me in the first place, I can't watch him *all* the time."

My mother queried Pete, "Burt never does anything that makes you uncomfortable, does he."

"Like what?"

"He never walks around naked, does he."

"He doesn't ever touch you, does he."

Later, she would remember the rhetorical way in which she phrased her questions so that the presumed answer would be no. Tag questions are highly suggestive, and punctuation changes the meaning.

He doesn't ever touch you, does he.

He doesn't ever touch you, does he?

A few weeks after the camping trip, Burt's accounting firm transferred him to Simi Valley, one hundred miles north, and my mother's worries disappeared with the threat. Tom and Lance lost touch after a few awkward phone calls.

About six months later, my mother came home to find Tom and Lance watching television. At first, she didn't recognize the boy. Children are said to have grown or bloomed, but rarely are they said to have aged. Lance looked as if he had aged. His eyes had sunk further into his already concave face, as if the water table that had kept his eyes afloat had dried up.

"Are you visiting?" my mother asked.

"My father got a new job, so we moved back."

The invitations started again. Burt was having a campfire on the beach. Burt had tickets to Lion Country Safari. Burt had free passes to the water park.

"I don't like to get wet," Pete said after my mother got off the phone with Burt and asked if he wanted to go.

"Since when don't you like to get wet?"

"I don't feel good."

She touched his forehead to see if it was hot.

"My stomach hurts."

She asked if it was something he ate.

"I can't go to the bathroom."

"Number one or number two?"

"Two."

"For how long?"

"I don't remember. Maybe Sunday?"

"After the sleepover at Burt's?"

Pete guessed that sounded right. Burt's daughter was at her grandmother's, he guessed.

"The daughter wasn't there? Who did you play with?"

"Burt."

This time she did not phrase the question so that the presumed answer was no. "Does Burt ever touch you?"

Pete nodded.

15

A STUDENT AT CALARTS, A YOUNG WOMAN WHO PAINTED AB-
stract landscapes, went missing around the same time. Her abandoned
car and easel had been found by the side of a dirt road in Box Canyon,
not far from Spahn Ranch, where the Manson family had been arrested
only three years before. I knew the area. It was high school chic to hike
the ranch looking for Manson family artifacts.

The passenger door of her Beetle had been left open, and her palette and brushes were on the front seat. An oil painting of the canyon,
face up in the dirt, was still tacky. Oil paint dries over several days. The
police were able to determine that her abduction had taken place forty-
eight hours before.

The art office was temporarily turned into police central as detectives commandeered the dean's office to interview the missing student's
friends. My new work-study job was to stop potential witnesses from
talking to each other while they waited in the hall. On the day my
mother reached me at school, hysterical and threatening to kill Burt,
two weeks had passed since the young woman's disappearance, and
that afternoon, the police had brought in a psychic. She looked noth-

ing like the card table gypsies on Venice Beach. She wore a business suit and pumps.

It was difficult to understand what my mother was trying to tell me between her garbled sobs and the flat pitch of the psychic's voice as she methodically described what she saw in her mind's eye: "I see a shallow grave that has already been pillaged by animals. I see a flat desert with no tire tracks."

On the phone, my mother floundered between self-recrimination and revenge. She kept berating herself for having taken so long to act on her suspicions. She had asked Pete the right questions but in the wrong way. Tonight, she planned to wait outside Burt's house in her Fiat and then run him over in his driveway. If she called the police, Pete would have to testify.

Eyes shut, the psychic was now holding the painting found face up in the dirt. She had taken off the exhibit bag so that she could explore the surface unimpeded by plastic. I was only a few feet away, leashed to the reception desk by the phone cord.

As the psychic ran her fingers lightly over the surface, a planchette around a Ouija board, she said, "She has visited the canyon before. There are other paintings, but this one is different. It wasn't painted where it was found. There is another painting underneath, but I can't see what it is."

She sighed, opened her eyes, and shrugged.

After I hung up and asked the dean's assistant if I could be excused for a family emergency, the psychic looked over at me as if she had meant to speak to me all along.

"I don't know if I should say this to you," she said to me, "but I feel some kind of connection. Not between you and Judith [the missing girl] but between whatever your family is going through and Box Canyon."

Arnold drove me to my mother's house. It was rush hour on the 405, and I was too shaken to drive. My mother had reached Arnold before phoning me at school. He had urged her to call the police, and when my frantic mother choked out her biggest fear, that Pete would have to testify, he assured her that Pete would be under no obligation to appear in court.

Two detectives, both in creased suits, were in the living room interviewing my mother when we arrived.

"Where's Pete?" I asked.

Before my mother could answer, the detective nosing around the family memorabilia arranged on the coffee table said, "He's in his room."

"Jack and Tom are with him," my mother said. Her voice had lost its natural intonations. She sounded like the voice you heard when you phoned to learn the current time.

The other detective, the one taking notes on a steno pad, asked Arnold, "Are you the boy's father?"

"No."

"What is your relationship to Pete?"

Arnold could hardly say that he was Pete's brother-in-law. "A friend of the family."

"You'll have to wait outside," the detective said.

"I want him here," my mother said.

The dining room table was requisitioned by the detectives while we were asked to wait in my mother's bedroom until we were called. Tom was first. Earlier that afternoon, he had returned from school to find our mother rushing Pete to the ER. When he asked why, she told him that Pete had been molested by Burt. She pressed Tom the same direct way she had Pete: "Does Burt ever touch you?" Tom swore Burt had never put a hand on him, that he never saw Burt hurt Pete, that he would never let anyone hurt Pete.

Later, my mother would describe to me the Herculean effort it took her not to ask Tom the question tormenting her. *How could you not have known?*

Now the police were asking her middle son that very question, planting doubt about the integrity of his love for Pete. She worried Tom would blame himself, as she blamed herself. She could now see how blind she had been, how her saleswoman's optimism, her live-and-let-live attitude, her stubborn need to trust people, had harmed her sons—yes, sons, both Tom and Pete.

When Tom returned, it was obvious he had been crying. He asked my mother if he had to go to school tomorrow. She told him he didn't. Could he transfer schools? He never wanted to see Lance again.

Pete was next. My mother asked if she could be with him during the interview.

"You'll have to refrain from answering questions for him," the detective said.

She asked Pete, "Do you want me there?"

"Not yet," Pete said.

As soon as the detective closed the door behind him and Pete, my mother pressed her ear against the wall adjacent to the dining room.

"What are they saying?" I asked.

"I can't make out Pete's answers."

Jack brought my mother an empty drinking glass he found in her bathroom. She held it against the wall, rim down, and listened.

By the contortions my mother's face assumed, we guessed she could now hear Pete's answers. She lowered the glass. "I can't bear this. Someone else listen."

Jack took the glass, but he didn't hold it against the wall. He cupped it in his hands, looking down into it, as if he couldn't bear to drink whatever it contained. He handed it to me.

It took a few adjustments, but I finally heard the detective's voice.

"What did he ask you to measure his penis with?"

"A ruler, what else would I have used?"

I gave the glass back to Jack, who returned it to the bathroom, where it remained for the duration of Pete's interview.

After the detectives left, my mother sat deep in her peacock chair, knees up, fingers locked around the orange pom-pom pillow. The chair was the only relic to survive the family's move. She said she wasn't ready to face Pete, who waited in his and Tom's bedroom. She worried that if Pete saw how terminally shaken she was, it would only confirm the magnitude of what happened to him. But she also worried that if we behaved as if nothing happened, if we turned on the television, say, he would think no one cared.

Arnold finally rose from the sofa and tapped on Pete's door, asking him what he wanted for dinner. Earlier, at the ER, a nurse had given Pete an enema, and he hadn't eaten all day.

Pete came out of his door. His parakeet, Gloria, was dancing on his shoulder. He asked for pizza.

As Arnold sat in his car in the Pizza Hut parking lot waiting for Pete's pie, the intensity of the afternoon's events must have been reverberating within him: the frantic call from Gloria, the paintbrushes he forgot to wash out in his rush to drive me, the sluggish traffic on the 405, the way the detectives had reacted to him when he first walked into Gloria's apartment with me. Their first question—"Are you the boy's father?"—momentarily surprised him, but their next question—"What is your relationship to the boy?"—only confirmed his suspicion. They thought he was Gloria's paramour. The paramour is always the prime suspect. By identifying himself as "a friend of the family" rather than the victim's sister's boyfriend, he had left their assumption to fester. Every time the detective came into Gloria's bedroom to retrieve a family member, he had given Arnold a look that said, *How do you fit into all this?* A little later, after Pete's interview and before the detectives left, I had started to cry and he held me. The intimacy of the embrace made it evident to the detectives that he was with me, not Gloria.

He remembered the way the two detectives exchanged glances.

The coincidence of two older men involved with the children of this household alarmed them. Did it alarm Arnold? Sleeping with a willing seventeen-year-old is in no way analogous to child molestation, yet he must have been aware that he, like Burt, had benefited from the vulnerability of fatherless children. I asked Arnold to rock me to sleep that night, just rock me.

———

What was going through Pete's head that night? What does it mean to be seven years old and realize that life is upheaval and no one is safe?

As Arnold rocked me, I tried to imagine how Pete would remember this day. He had finished the whole pizza by himself. He had been interviewed for close to an hour by adults he didn't know. My mother had put him to bed early. The interview must have stirred up memories, both random and beckoned. The electric racetrack that he and Burt had assembled on the living room floor. Holding Burt's hand on the skyway to Tomorrowland. Burt walking naked through the house. Burt asking him to measure his penis. He had wanted Burt's affections but not in that way. Do children feel the same disquieting and inexplicable culpability that date rape victims do? *You dressed up for him, you let him hold your hand, you let him take you to Disneyland.* Or was the rupture from childhood so seismic that he would not understand how it reconfigured him until years afterward?

———

My mother kept Tom and Pete home from school until Burt was arrested, which, according to the detectives, might take a few days. She drew the blinds and didn't let the boys outside. Helplessness mutated into fury. One night, she drove by Burt's house. Lance was wheeling out the garbage bin. She considered grabbing him, to interrogate him or to save him, she wasn't sure. Burt was on the upstairs deck, smoking a cigarette. The smug, deep inhalations he took with each drag made my mother believe that, at this very minute, he was contemplating another tryst with her seven-year-old son. She almost got out of the car to pick up a rock and throw it at him but drove to the beach instead. The noisy waves breaking against a pier's pilings riled her with their false drama. Around three a.m., unable to sleep, her rage incendiary, her body sweating, she phoned Burt. When his groggy, irked voice asked who was calling at this hour, my mother hissed (she didn't want to wake her sons) that she knew what he had done, that he would spend the rest of his life in jail, where, as a pervert, he would be raped and beaten daily and she wished on him only pain, and if she didn't think he was suffering enough, she would hire another prisoner to blind him.

In the morning, she told the detectives what she had done. By the time the police raided Burt's house later that afternoon, the family had fled, leaving behind most of their clothes and Lance's model airplane collection.

Were they a family? Was Burt really a divorced father with a son and a daughter? Or had Burt purchased Lance and the little girl? The hunt for him took over a month. He belonged to a national "community" of pedophiles, a predecessor to NAMBLA, the North American Man/Boy Love Association. Despite the name, most of Burt's ring did not necessarily prefer one sex over the other.

Childhood was their victims' only commonality. Girls couldn't get pregnant, so what was the harm? Burt and twenty-eight other men had pooled their money and rented a four-bedroom house in a Chatsworth subdivision near the entrance of Box Canyon, the place the psychic had warned me about. During the raid, police found hundreds of magazines (*Bambino Sex, Lollitots, Baby Love, Nudist Moppets*), a VCR camera (a technology the arresting officers had never seen before), a darkroom with dozens of copies of a single photograph (a naked Japanese boy) drying on clothespins, a mimeograph machine with a fresh René Guyon Society newsletter in the roller (their motto: "Sex before eight or else it's too late"), one file cabinet stuffed with mailing lists, another with letters from "pen pals," children as far away as Maine. Burt and nine others were swept up during the raid. He tried to escape out a bathroom window but surrendered when the police gave chase. There are no exits in Box Canyon.

The detectives went in person to inform my mother that Burt had been arrested and had confessed. Pete would not need to testify.

"How long will he get?" my mother asked.

"Ten to thirteen years."

My mother looked disappointed.

"It's a life sentence for a pervert in prison."

The taller of the two gave her the name of a counselor who specialized in sexually abused children. "You're lucky Pete is a boy," he told my mother as he was leaving. "Boys are always believed. Not that the girls aren't, it just takes longer."

Tom came out of his room after the front door closed.

"What happened to Lance?" he asked my mother.

"He's safe," she told him. Later she would tell me, "I didn't ask."

16

MY MOTHER SURREPTITIOUSLY STUDIED THE OLDER COUPLE, concave with grief, as they stood next to their dead daughter's paintings. The memorial exhibition opened the same evening as my BFA show. My senior project had been an autobiographical symphony played on a touch-tone phone, a relatively new technology in 1974. Headphones on, my mother sat on a bench straining not to act bored as she listened to a cassette tape of me dialing all the phone numbers of my life, when she suddenly was drawn to the man whose posture had been pithed of bone, and the woman whose reddened eyes kept searching for her daughter in the vast hall of milling faculty and students. Her daughter's skull had been found two months before by hikers in the Mojave Desert, yet the woman's darting eyes still maintained hope that her daughter might walk in.

I had met the Martins earlier that evening, escorted them to the gallery, a small annex normally reserved for visiting faculty shows adjacent to the main exhibition hall. The memorial exhibit had been my final work-study assignment before graduation. I had hung the paintings chronologically, except for the one of Box Canyon. The police were keeping it as evidence, though after nearly a year, all the trails had gone cold. I had hoped that by my hanging the landscapes chronologically the Martins would see how their daughter's last impressions of the physical world had matured from imitation to imagination. Aside from the Martins, the small gallery was empty.

"We should go in there," my mother said, taking off the headphones. "Someone should pay attention to their daughter's work." My mother had been following the case on the local news. The discovery of the skull had promised answers but only raised more questions. Had the young woman been kept alive for a period of time? How had her skull ended up in the desert?

My mother didn't immediately introduce herself to the Martins. She stood in front of each painting long enough to acknowledge the mind that had once occupied the skull. My mother believed in a hierarchy of suffering. Her son had lost his innocence, but their daughter had lost everything.

"Who's in charge here?" asked a man I recognized as the minimalist artist whose show had previously occupied the annex.

The Martins looked at each other. "It's our daughter's exhibition," Mr. Martin said.

"You've hung the paintings on top of my work."

The work he referred to was an environmental piece. Six weeks before, with a darker shade of white paint than the gallery walls, he had feathered the corners to create the illusion that the space had no edges. When the show ended, and I had taken down his artist statement, everyone assumed the gallery was empty. I had not seen any reason to paint over something that no one could see anyway.

Striding out, the artist said, "I'll be back."

"Your daughter was very talented," my mother said.

"We didn't want her to go to this school," Mrs. Martin said. "We live in Evanston. She should have gone to the Chicago Art Institute."

My mother stood in the center of the space and did a panoramic turn.

"You can see how she comes to love California," my mother said.

"Why would you say that?" Mrs. Martin asked.

"The colors," my mother said.

Mrs. Martin approached the paintings anew. The early landscapes were flat and monochromatic, but the later ones were flecked with prismatic light. My mother was right: Color had been introduced. Color is the language of dreams, according to Cézanne.

The conceptual artist returned with the assistant dean, the one who used to rub my shoulders while I typed.

"Do you see what I'm talking about?" The artist spoke to the assistant dean as if no one else was present. "It's insulting."

"We'll get a student to paint the gallery first thing tomorrow," the assistant dean said, looking at me.

"You find my daughter's paintings insulting?" Mr. Martin asked the artist.

"I find the act of desecrating one of my art pieces insulting, yes."

"What are you talking about? There is nothing there," Mrs. Martin said.

"It's hard to see in this light."

"Get out," Mr. Martin said.

His back to us, Arnold stood on the far side of the main gallery unaware of the confrontation in the annex. Earlier that evening, I had instructed him—a little too testily—not to stand beside me during *my* opening, that when a man stood beside a woman, especially an older man and a younger woman, the woman became invisible, except as an object of acquisition.

He was looking at a sketch of a woman who resembled the Mona Lisa. The placard beside the drawing explained that the artist had described Mona Lisa's features to a police sketch artist and this drawing was the result.

Arnold found conceptual art clever but cold. One of my teachers had burned his paintings and used the ashes to make cookies that he later ate in front of an audience. Arnold could never eat his paintings, even the failures. It would have been like eating his children. The only work in the show that he admired were the dead girl's paintings.

He walked into the annex to find a tableau vivant—me, my mother, and the Martins, paralyzed by anguish, in edgeless space.

"I was just telling the Martins how their daughter's paintings had become more colorful," my mother said, desperate to end the deafening silence.

Arnold approached the last painting, dated a week before the abduction, a landscape with cows. "It wasn't so much that she added surface color but that she learned to underpaint with color," he said.

The Martins didn't appear to hear him at first, but then Mrs. Martin broke the tableau and challenged him.

"Do you think we're stupid?" she asked. "First we are told that there is an invisible piece of artwork under our daughter's paintings and now you are telling us there is another painting under the cows. My daughter loved cows. Why can't cows just be cows?"

———

Michelle's twenty-first birthday shared the weekend with my BFA show. Arnold wanted to celebrate her milestone by taking her out for her first cocktail to Musso and Frank's, an old Hollywood restaurant decorated with framed caricatures of movie stars who had patronized the garnet-red booths over the years. The bow-tie-sporting waiters were all in their seventh or eighth decade. I had turned twenty-one two months before, so I was legal. But I would need to remember to behave as if I was twenty-four and not bring up my graduation or my first cocktail, a mai tai I had sipped in this very restaurant only eight weeks before.

Michelle asked Arnold what she should order.

"I would skip the dry martini," he said.

When she stopped laughing, she asked me what I was ordering.

"Do you like sweet drinks?" I asked.

She did.

I suggested a mai tai.

As we waited for the elderly waiter to bring us our cocktails, Michelle looked at the caricature of Kirk Douglas on the wall above her and said, "He looks like someone shot a hole in his chin."

"The cleft is what gives him his million-dollar face," Arnold said.

"Why does he look so crazy?"

"It's a caricature. The artist exaggerated the features on purpose so that you'll feel something about the subject. What do you feel?"

"I can't tell if he is handsome or ugly."

"What else?"

"The artist liked him."

"Why do you say that?"

"Why else would he have drawn him? Will you draw one of me?"

"A caricature?"

"Yes."

Arnold reached for the pen he always kept in the front pocket of his jeans, though over the years, hundreds of pens had dug their way to freedom though an escape hole in the fabric.

He smoothed out his cocktail napkin while Michelle posed. The pose was nothing like I had been anticipating, the pose I myself might have taken—chin up, a sly smile, my best side. Michelle's pose looked as if she had anticipated how her father would exaggerate her features and then arranged them that way.

Arnold made his first mark. The pen's direction, up or down the paper, is important. When the nib first presses against the sheet, the mark is thicker. The line that follows is a tapering arrow. All Arnold's first marks pointed upward, giving the portrait a regal bearing, though Michelle slouched deeper in the red booth.

I watched Arnold's pen point as he drew her eyes and then added ink to each pupil, transforming her timorous stare into one of confidence. He straightened out her knitted brows. Michelle looked like herself, but a prettier self who had agency.

Arnold's drawings normally skewed toward the grotesque. He naturally drew the shadows of the world, not the light. Even a quick sketch on a napkin was never about flattery for him, but it was that evening.

When he showed Michelle the results, her exaggerated expression softened into genuine elation. I could see how pleased Arnold was by her reaction. I understood, in a way I had not before, how unconditionally he loved this troubled woman-child, that his love for her was no less profound than Mr. Martin's for his daughter. It shocked me.

17

I LOST FAITH IN CONCEPTUAL ART SHORTLY AFTER MY GRADUA-
tion. What had once seemed profound and prescient now struck me
as dull and flat. It had taken me four years to master the obfuscating
language of the avant-garde—the jargon and the in-jokes—and now
it sounded like pig Latin to me. I was no less surprised and anguished
about the loss than a believer who realized that she was alone, utterly
alone; He wasn't there.

My doubts about conceptual art had been seeded in me during my
senior year. Was newness the point of art? Experimentation? Clever-
ness? Shock? Was it the artist's duty to rush ahead of humanity and
report back from the future? If there was an advance guard, were we at
war? Who was the enemy? But my first awareness that faith had abandoned me happened the night of my BFA show. I had left my mother
unattended in the crowded exhibition hall to escort the Martins to
their daughter's memorial show. When I returned, I was reeking of
their grief. My mother was unaware of my presence. She was studying one of the student artworks—animal organs nailed to a wall in the
shape of a lamb. Her face told me what I already knew. If art were a
conversation, which I believed it was, this work wasn't interested in

hearing what my mother had to say. This art didn't care that she had once ridden a streetcar to the museum during a snowstorm to stand in front of Gauguin's *Are You Jealous?* and let herself be transported to Tahiti and join in the ongoing conversation (which includes those who have died and those who haven't yet been born) about who is jealous of whom.

I considered returning to drawing and painting, but feared I would become Arnold's lifelong apprentice, forever mired in the emergent state of *promising*. He had not only taught me how to draw; he had taught me how to see. I would forever perceive the physical world through the veneer of his interpretation.

During his own crisis of faith, when he had let his paints go dry for a decade, he had written a novel, a Henry Miller–like romp about a middle-aged artist who sleeps with his models. An editor at Knopf had encouraged him, but after three drafts and no contract, Arnold put it away. Soon after we became lovers, he gave me the pages and asked if I agreed with his editor's criticisms. At seventeen, I thought the novel was marvelous just as it was.

I read it again, this time with the cold critical eye of a twenty-one-year-old. The tone wasn't at all as I remembered it—droll and wise. The narration was therapeutic and the story indulgent in a way that his paintings never were. I might never paint as brilliantly as him, but I knew I could tell a more original story.

When I told Arnold and my mother that I was going to become a writer, my mother said to him, "But she's never written anything, not even a book report. She doesn't know what a run-on sentence is. She can't spell *cat*."

This was true.

Whenever I had tried to write, the letters came out upside down, or backward, or in the wrong order. I could draw anything and everything except language.

That night, Arnold sat me down at his typewriter because he could see that holding a pencil had prompted me to confuse handwriting with drawing. He assured me that if I could learn to draw, I could learn to write. His unshakable confidence in my intellect quieted my terrors. An age-appropriate boyfriend might have told me the same things, but I would not have believed him.

Arnold asked me to read aloud from the fledgling story I had been writing. Each time I paused for a beat, he had me insert a comma. He explained that a clause was only the number of words you could string between commas, and I had to be careful not to hang too many words or the string would break. He showed me how tenses were to language what perspective was to painting. Tenses made a story three-dimensional. *Had* was further back in time than *was,* and *is* existed only on the surface. He introduced me to adjectives by calling them language's colors. Adjectives gave a noun mood, as pigment gave a tone spirit.

He was patient and practiced. After all, he had already raised a learning-disabled daughter.

18

I HAD NOT SEEN OR SPOKEN TO MY FATHER IN SIX YEARS WHEN he appeared unannounced in my hospital room. I pretended to be asleep. Two days before, I had a partial hysterectomy to remove an infected ovary. I was twenty-three.

Arnold had never met my father. I kept no pictures of him.

"Can I help you?" Arnold asked.

"Is this my daughter's room?"

"Who is your daughter?"

"Her," my father said.

With my eyes shut, I could not tell which man remained at the foot of my hospital bed and which man came to my bedside. Only after I felt a kiss on my forehead did I smell my father's pipe tobacco. My father had never kissed me before.

"When is she going to wake up?" my father asked.

"She just had major surgery," Arnold said.

"Her mother told me she was in the hospital."

"Did she tell you Jill can't have children?"

"Did she want children?"

"She said she didn't, but how could she know at twenty-three?"

I knew. I had never wanted children. I had known this about myself ever since I was a child, as another child might know she is gay.

I could sense my father's disquiet.

"Let me tell you about your daughter," Arnold said. He bragged to my father about all the gold stars I had earned at CalArts. He described my bravery and determination to become a writer. He talked one father to another. Did Arnold see the irony of this? He must have wished someone would talk to him about Michelle in such a hopeful, confident way.

It was quiet for a moment before my father spoke. "She must get it from me." The smell of pipe tobacco receded. "I'll come back and see her tomorrow," he said.

I did not hear from my father again for another ten years, not until he was lying in his own hospital bed.

But that afternoon, as Arnold walked him out, I chanced a look at the two of them—short, gray-haired, middle-aged Jewish men born two months apart.

19

PHOTOGRAPHS OF US FROM THE MID-'70S—MY TWENTIES, AR-
nold's fifties—did not look as scandalous as earlier pictures, any of
which could have served as the paperback jacket for *Lolita*. The age
difference is still wildly apparent, but it is no longer the only thing one
sees.

We were now the same height, five foot six. I had still been growing
when we met. I had to raise my lips for our first kiss.

Now we kissed straight on.

Our clothes style was similar. Early on, we had to choose whose generational dress code we would observe, and I won. Arnold gave up his straight-legged slacks for bell-bottom jeans, and his tweed jackets, with the customary suede patches on the elbows, for a bomber jacket. I updated his hairstyle, clipped the rabbinical curls from his beard. He was a handsome man—graying with just the right photogenic blend of black and white. Now that I was in charge of his wardrobe, he did not look *that* old.

But what about when he was nude?

Nudity is different than nakedness. To be naked is to be oneself. To be nude is to be seen naked by others. In Arnold's life drawing classes, I did not learn to draw a naked body; I learned to draw a nude. He taught me to seek out the body's imperfections and irregularities to make my drawings dynamic and original. When I looked at Arnold's fifty-five-year-old body as he stepped out of the shower or lowered himself on top of me, the physical imperfections—the loose skin, the extra flesh, all that six decades does to a body—made me feel as if our love was dynamic and original.

Soon after I came home from the hospital, we moved from the rental house overlooking the Hollywood Freeway to a storefront on Crenshaw Boulevard, in the shadow of another freeway, the 10, which cleaved White LA from Black. Artists had recently moved into the area to take advantage of the low rents. A lit frosted storefront window at night usually meant an artist was living illegally in their studio. The fire inspector periodically conducted surprise raids to catch the culprits and evict them.

The illicit, risqué lifestyle suited my fantasies of how artists and writers should live. But Arnold must have known better. He was on the unkind side of middle age. He taught figure drawing classes five days a week and painted at night. I must have been an exhausting twenty-five-year-old with all my hormones and ambitions and self-doubts colliding and sparking. From time to time, he must have yearned to return to his former life—the three-bedroom ranch house, the comfortable savings account, all that he had given up for me. Was he so gullible that he believed a twenty-five-year-old's fantasies? Was his yearning to be young again so extreme that he had been willing to start over for me?

I did not yet understand what starting over truly meant at his age. All I knew was that *he* was willing to learn from *me*, that I had something to teach.

The store we rented had once been a beauty parlor, and there was a drain every ten feet in the cement floor. A curtain divided the rear living space from the studio, but we rarely closed it. His paintings were everywhere, in any case. I was living inside his mind.

He shunned tubes and painted out of buckets. He would dip the golden horsehair bristles of his brush (the size you would use to paint a fence) into a pail of, say, alizarin crimson (the consistency of unset pudding), and then race over to the spot on the canvas he had just been studying. After he made a stroke or a stab, he would jump back to see how the new shape transfigured the whole. Back and forth, microscopic and cosmic, comets of pigment trailing behind his brushes. He only stopped after he reached an egalitarian distribution of frenetic color. He believed consistency of surface was more crucial than bravado.

Next, he lined up buckets of diluted color. With grapefruit-size sea sponges, he splashed the painting's surface with the dirty water again and again until the image was submerged in murk. After the glazes dried, he coaxed the image out of the darkness with varnish and rubbing alcohol. What was left was intrinsic color, *eigengrau,* what you see on the back of your eyelids.

While he taught figure drawing classes, I modeled in the nude for his students. Holding poses that accentuated the female form, I would listen to him instruct his students on how to draw my body. "Her buttocks are round forms, not flat shapes. Her breasts don't ride on top of the rib cage, they spill over it." Rather than being mortified at having my nudity described, it gave me an erotic charge.

While he painted at night, I wrote short stories in bed, a mattress on a plywood model stand. I typed sentence after sentence trying to find my voice, as if a voice were a penny you could lose. Despite Arnold's assurances, learning to write was not at all like learning to draw. To draw, I needed to open my eyes wide; to write, I needed to shut them tightly and turn the gaze on my naked self.

We were both in a fervent state of uncharted creativity—me for the first time, him for the second. We pulled all-nighters and still managed to make love afterward. We critiqued each other's work—brutally, lavishly, meticulously—not as teacher and pupil, but as collaborators. If I saw something lacking in his painting, I would pick up a brush and make my corrections directly on the canvas. If he read a digression in my story that petered out, he would excise it with a thick pencil stroke. Sometimes I would cry and rip up all my pages, but he would invariably collect the shreds out of the wastebasket and tape them back together.

Where did Arnold get his energy? From me, of course. But please don't equate this with an old vampire drinking a maiden's lifeblood. To offer someone you love energy when you are practically bursting with it feels heady and magnanimous.

20

1982. I TURNED TWENTY-NINE, ARNOLD SIXTY. IN BORROWED
winter coats, buffeted by icy gusts blasting off the Hudson, we struggled to keep his painting, an unstretched six-foot canvas rolled around
a cardboard tube, balanced on his shoulder. Transporting the painting from Los Angeles to New York on the red-eye had been my idea.
A gallerist on West Broadway had expressed gushing enthusiasm for
Arnold's imagery, but she could not commit to a show from the photographs alone. She would need to see the originals. She had promised
to fly to LA for a studio visit but had to cancel twice. As weeks turned
into months, I encouraged him to take a painting with him to New
York and wrest back control.

What the gallerist had not been able to see from the photographs
alone was how Arnold handled paint, the ridges and whorls of pigment
that are as individual as fingerprints. Arnold's saturated brushstrokes
crested and roiled like the ocean's surface. Whatever lived unseen
beneath filled the viewer with awe and fear.

The gallery was on the fourth floor of a factory building that had
recently been converted to retail. The gallerist, a crusty fifty-something

woman with the kindest eyes, had not met Arnold in person before, only spoken to him over the phone. When we first walked in, I saw surprise in her face. As Arnold and she shook hands, I could see her recalibrating her response.

After introductions, Arnold and I unrolled the canvas on the floor, and she slowly walked around it. The imagery was a night scene, two naked men wrestling under a traffic light. She tilted her head this way and that, and then asked if we could hold it up.

Arnold and I each lifted a corner of the canvas and held it above our heads.

"Does it have a title?" she asked.

"*Gridlock*," Arnold said.

She approached the painting, lightly touched the surface. "Oil?"

"Acrylic," Arnold said.

She motioned that we could lay down the painting again.

"You're a great painter," she told Arnold. She had her assistant bring us coffee, but she did not take a seat, so neither did we. "Suppose I took you on. The first thing I would need to do is put you in a group show. The gallery is booked through June '84. It might take another year before I could give you a one-man show. I wouldn't want to open without red dots next to at least two-thirds of the paintings. Half dots just scream indecision. Can I be completely honest with you?" Her eyes no longer looked kind. "When my assistant showed me your images last summer, I told her, 'This kid is really going somewhere.' You're too old to invest in."

"Am I too old?" Arnold asked me. He was resting on a park bench in Tompkins Square after stubbornly shouldering his rolled painting for ten city blocks, though I had offered to take one end. I sat down beside him and took his hand. How do you comfort someone when the source of their anguish is inconceivable to you?

"She doesn't know what she is talking about," I said. "Had Goya thrown in his brushes at your age, he would never have painted his Black Paintings. There would be no *Drowning Dog*."

Arnold revered Goya. He ranked the Black Paintings as Goya's masterpieces and *The Drowning Dog* as Goya's most beautiful work—a desperate little gray-muzzled dog appears to plead for help, submerged up to its neck in a choppy sea.

"Goya never called it *The Drowning Dog*," Arnold said. "He never intended that any of the Black Paintings be seen, let alone gave them titles. He was seventy-three and deaf. He painted them as murals on the walls of his farmhouse. The dog was probably the last image he painted before he died. A profiteering baron bought the farmhouse and had the paintings transferred to canvas. He made up the titles."

Arnold fell silent. I asked if he was cold, if he wanted to go back to the hotel.

"The dog isn't drowning," he said. "It's paddling."

———

I had heard about a new gallery scene in the East Village, just east of the park, where the art was said to be eclectic and raw.

"You carried the painting this far," I said. "Let's try another gallery. What do you have to lose?"

"My dignity," Arnold said.

The first gallery we entered, on the corner of 11th Street and Avenue B, was a reconfigured ice cream parlor called Civilian Warfare. The space was not twelve feet wide and congested with art—dozens of self-portraits, each by a different artist, painted on broken mirrors.

A man with flamboyant hair, another with bad skin and piercings, and a woman with a shaved head sat on stools smoking cigarettes. They were not more than a few years younger than me, but they were of a different generation. I could see their amusement at the old bearded artist carrying his rolled painting—like a cross—from gallery to gallery.

"Okay to leave this here while we look around?" Arnold asked, leaning his painting against the front window, the only surface absent of art.

I need to emphasize here that not only was Arnold drawn to youth, but that youth was drawn to Arnold. Within minutes, he vanquished their bemused expressions with the intensity of his concentration: He did not so much look at art as dissect it. He walked from portrait to portrait, cocked his head this way and that, leaned close enough to observe the paint's microscopic application, the opacity of the glazes, the transition from one value to another, and then stepped back to see the whole. The energy he exuded was massively out of alignment with his age, and that was what fascinated young people. Arnold promised wisdom without the loss of vitality.

The boy with flamboyant hair asked what he thought of the work.

Arnold said he respected the art's rebelliousness but thought some of the artists were too cautious when it came to technique. He pointed to a highlight on one of the subject's cheeks. "The paint is feathered to create form. Illustrators do that, not artists."

I would learn the gallerists' stories later, but I did not need the specifics to recognize the type. As they helped Arnold unroll his painting on the floor, as they gathered around him to learn how he was able to make acrylic look as juicy as oil, it was so apparent to me that they were looking for a father themselves.

I felt a tinge of jealousy. Was I being replaced?

Arnold was offered his first New York exhibition. I had started my first novel and found a literary agent who wanted to represent it. We decided to move to New York City for six months, forever if we could get a foothold. The only glitch was Michelle.

She had recently moved back in with her mother after a "tough love" experiment ended with her living in her car. Arnold wanted Michelle to get a job before we left. He believed it was her best chance at a meaningful life, but I understood that it was his best chance for escape. He had not yet told her that we were moving to New York; that he had found a gallery to represent him; that he and I were going to paint and write by day, dance at the clubs by night; that he was abandoning her to find a meaningful life on her own.

He asked me to help her write a résumé. If he tried, they would only end up arguing.

Michelle arrived at the back door of our storefront on Crenshaw, holding a three-ring binder thick with loose papers. She still wore granny dresses, but where they had once suggested kinship in a tribe, they now suggested exile. We had both reached the age—thirty—where our choices started to show. The triangular chin she had inherited from her father had doubled and was now round. Her listening expression was no longer bafflement but wiliness.

She had been homeless for two months before her mother caved. I knew her itinerary by the collect calls Arnold had accepted. Carpinteria, Ventura, Oxnard, any beach town tolerant of people sleeping in their cars.

Our back door opened onto a parking lot, and I noticed her car next to the station wagon with four flats. The wagon had taken root long before we moved in. A homeless vet named Walter kept a mattress in the rear. Our next-door neighbor, the fish fry's owner, an ex-marine, let Walter use the restaurant's bathroom and cashed his government checks for him.

"Who lives in that car?" Michelle asked before coming inside.

"His name is Walter," I said.

"Where does he go to the bathroom?"

I feared why she was asking.

"I don't know," I lied.

As we sat across from each other at the dining table, I could not shake the unsettling feeling that her misfortunes were in inverse proportion to my good luck; that every time another gram of trouble was removed from my side of the scale, she sank lower.

She opened the binder I had asked her to prepare—former jobs, the dates of employment, her responsibilities. Instead of a list, she had written a journal about her twenties. Michelle had spent the last decade drifting—not exactly in circles, because geometry suggests order, but down aimless paths she vaguely recognized only after she had gotten lost. The handwriting was childlike. No two entries had been written with the same pen or pencil. Most did not fit on the page, so she had continued on the back, attaching her thoughts with arrows flying up and down the margins.

"Are these chronological?" I asked.

"I included my babysitting experience, but I don't want to work with children anymore."

"What years did you babysit?"

"1973 and '74, in June or July, I think."

"Your next job isn't until '77."

"I couldn't remember the exact date, but I remember the name, Little Stars Academy Preschool."

The entry didn't include the length of employment. Only the day she had been hired.

"How long did you work there?" I asked.

"It says."

"One day?"

"The woman who owned the nursery school and I didn't agree about childcare practices."

The rest of the pages were blank. I finished typing her résumé—thirteen weeks of employment in eight years—and walked her to her car.

Walter was sitting on his tailgate. He asked for a cigarette, and Michelle offered him her whole pack. Then, standing closer to him than I would have braved, she patiently burned through one match after another before his trembling hands stilled the cigarette long enough to catch fire.

Who would love this generous, indolent, lost woman-child after her mother and Arnold were gone? Me?

————

Arnold called my mother that evening. "Gloria, please hire her."

My mother had been married twice by then, but Arnold was the longest-standing man in her life. He, not my father, had attended her daughter's and sons' graduations. He had cosigned the mortgage for her condo when the bank refused to gamble on a single mother. She promised him that she would find a job for Michelle in her salon.

My mother was having her own renaissance. Tired of working for others, she had opened her own business, G. J. International Body Wraps. She had rented the back room of a strip mall nail salon, acquired a used massage table from the *PennySaver* classifieds, repaired a tear in the table's white faux-leather cushion with liquid paper, and asked Arnold to help her hang her beloved Gauguin poster of two Tahitian women, hefty but free of cellulite, on the wall above her desk.

The first six months had been iffy. After she bought the cellulite cream and the expensive individual wraps, two-foot squares of transparent film, her profit margin was low. She experimented on herself, diluted the cellulite cream with cold cream, replaced the individual wraps with cellophane. Her customers preferred the cellophane. She added a display case and filled it with weight-loss products she found in the *National Enquirer*—a wristband that suppressed appetite, bath salts that absorbed fat, a sauna suit, and what was to become her biggest seller, the Stomach Machine, a small plastic box with a science-fiction instrument panel and eight electric pads. Attached to your torso, the pads caused your stomach muscles to exercise without any effort on your part.

At fifty-five, my mother had finally become cognizant of her unique gift. She didn't sell wraps or bath salts; she sold time-shares in her bullishly optimistic worldview. The women arrived early for their appointments so that they had extra time to tell my mother their troubles, and they stayed late so that they could hear how my mother would fix their lives.

The day Michelle was to begin learning how to do body wraps, she didn't show. My mother waited until late morning before calling Michelle's house to see if she was all right. She had hesitated in case Michelle's mother answered. When Rose said hello, my mother introduced herself as Michelle's boss, but both women knew who the other was. Rose apologized for her daughter's behavior and promised that Michelle would call my mother as soon as she woke up.

Michelle called my mother just before midnight and said she didn't think the job was a good fit. No one called Arnold. It was three in the morning in New York. We would not have been home, in any case. We were dancing at the Palladium while Michelle returned to her childhood bedroom.

21

THE WORD *DEALER* HAD A DOUBLE MEANING IN THE EAST VIL-
lage. Limousines cruised for both drugs and art. We sublet a loft on
Avenue C, walking distance from the gallery. Arnold's new dealer,
the boy with flamboyant hair, was a charismatic twenty-four-year-old
impresario whose star burned bright enough to illuminate the dark
dicey neighborhood and make the art collectors feel safe in his presence. He would be dead of AIDS before he turned thirty. His gallery
was the hive around which a collective of twenty-something artists and
critics congregated. They were political, queer, and touchingly idealis-
tic. Their art had a catch-as-catch-can urgency, as if they already sensed
that a quarter of them would also be dead before thirty. Arnold was
treated as an elder. The jealousy I had experienced the first time I wit-
nessed their adoration of Arnold had only intensified when I saw his
paternal tenderness for them.

Arnold had been found while I had become lost.

My novel was stuck one hundred pages in. I had not been able to
commit a word to paper since we had moved to New York six months
before. Sometimes a writer gets stuck because she is at a loss as to what

comes next. Sometimes a writer knows too much about what comes next and is paralyzed by her own puny prophecies.

I was both.

My novel was about a sixteen-year-old girl who falls in love with a forty-seven-year-old man, the tired plot of countless novels and films by middle-aged men in the second half of the twentieth century. My twist was that I would tell the story from the teenage girl's point of view. The first titillating chapters had come easily. In my fictional account, the older man sleeps with the mother before the daughter has a chance to seduce him. I guess I thought the age difference wasn't risqué enough. In any case, the teenager and the old man's improbable love story somehow rights itself and . . .

I could not imagine how the story would end.

Lolita and Humbert Humbert marry and live happily ever after? Who would believe such a story? Who would believe a scene in which Lolita takes Humbert Humbert for cataract surgery? Or worries about his prostate? How would I compose the scene where Lolita arranges hospice care for the man who supposedly stole her childhood? Wouldn't I have to include the day Lolita is at Humbert Humbert's bedside when he dies? Isn't that what *happily ever after* means? A love that lasts long enough that one lover is there to close the other lover's eyelids?

The gallery invitations for Arnold's first exhibition had been printed and delivered to our sublet, five hundred oversize postcards of two men wrestling under a streetlight. Normally, Arnold and I would have addressed the invitations by hand, a task that took days, but I had offered the use of my new computer, a Macintosh 128K with a porthole-size screen and the memory of an old woman.

The computer had been the riskiest financial investment I had yet made in my career, which consisted of one published short story and a casual commitment from a literary agent to represent a novel I could not finish. Since moving to New York, the computer had sat idle, morning after morning, while I stared at the blinking cursor below the last sentence that I had managed to type before I went rigid. Time and again, the sentence had contorted, retched, sickened, died, rotted, yet a mysterious bud of life kept reappearing, shaming me from abandoning it.

Before I left that morning to teach Western Civilization to fashion students (a job I got because I was the only person to apply), I showed Arnold how to feed the crack-and-peel label sheets into my dot matrix printer, which required continuous adjustments lest it jam.

When I returned later that afternoon, hoarse and dispirited from my poor stage performance as a teacher who knew what she was talking about, Arnold sat at the dining table, sticking newly printed labels on the back of his invitations. As I watched him peel off the next sticker, I noticed that a portion of the address had remained behind. He had not correctly positioned the sheets into the feed and five hundred addresses were out of alignment.

"I warned you about the printer. I asked you to pay attention." I reached for the invitation he had just labeled. "Look! The zip code has been cut off. You're a half an inch out of alignment."

"I'm just a sixteenth of an inch off and I thought we could fill in the missing information later."

"How are we going to know which zip belongs to what person?"

"We can use my rolodex."

"For five hundred labels?"

I could tell he wasn't listening. His attention had been arrested by the reproduction of his painting on the flip side of the invite. He had struggled for months deciding what to paint under the streetlight before he hit on the two naked wrestlers—*l'affinité élective*, the belief that certain images have a hidden affinity.

"I'm worried I made a mistake," he said.

"You think?"

"Did I choose the right painting for the announcement?"

"I'd be more worried about the labels if I were you."

"Maybe that Soho dealer was right. Maybe I am too old."

"Too old to remember to watch the printer."

"We can print them again."

By the time I wrote another sentence, my new printer would be secondhand.

"Not on my machine."

He gave me the invitation with the missing zip code, as if I would know what to do with it. I crumpled it up and tossed it into the trash can.

"What are you doing?" He picked up the balled wad and tried to iron it flat with his palms.

What I really wanted to say but couldn't because it sounded to me then, as it sounds to me now, callow and sour and selfish, was: *You are old and I am young and it should be my turn.*

Instead, I said, "I hope no one comes to your opening."

I slammed the bedroom door behind me. I heard him leave a few minutes later.

Close to midnight, my mother called to tell me that she had just spoken to Arnold. He had called her from a pay phone on Canal Street and West Broadway, a particularly windy corner. It was early March, in the single digits. He would have needed to remove his gloves to manipulate the coins. Of late, the cold had turned his fingertips white and unresponsive.

"He is getting a second chance at sixty-two, have some compassion," my mother said. "He may be old enough to be your father, but remember, he isn't your parent. He does not love you unconditionally."

The painting Arnold selected for the announcement of his second show, only six months after the success of his first, was titled *The Fortress*—two larger-than-life doll heads, lit from within like Halloween pumpkins, stand sentry over a house of cards. The invitations arrived the morning he woke up blind.

He had undergone cataract surgery on his right eye the month before, and on his left only yesterday. After the first operation, light ricocheted off objects and the brilliance of cloudlessness made him want to paint outdoors. His right eye now saw colors he only remembered. For some time, he had been mixing his paints by recipe, not taste. Two cups cadmium red to one cup cobalt blue makes crimson. He had forgotten how lustrous crimson was, how complicated red could be. He called his new eye "my Impressionist eye" and couldn't wait to fix the other, which he now called his Rembrandt eye for its candle wattage and shadows.

"Should we call an ambulance?" I asked.

"I'm blind, not crippled. I can manage the stairs if you guide me," he said.

Our loft was on the fifth floor of a walk-up. The stairwell had no natural light, and the tenants were responsible for replacing burnt-out bulbs on their landings, but the tenant on the third floor had fought with the tenant above him and now both refused the other working lights. In the dark, Arnold and I had to navigate by feel alone. But Arnold's blindness felt blacker than mine. He clutched my arm tightly and stepped hesitantly, while I charged toward the light like a mineshaft mule out of a cave-in.

After shining a wand of light into Arnold's left pupil, the ophthalmologist told us that a stitch has come loose. Arnold would need emergency surgery to stop the bleeding.

"But why is his other eye blind?" I asked.

"In sympathy," the doctor said.

Both eyes needed rest and stability after the stitch was resewn. Arnold was told to remain in bed for ten days, head elevated, while wearing gauze and opaque eye shields.

In the taxi home, he asked, "What if I never see again?"

"The doctor said the surgery went well."

"I don't trust him. When I complained that my right eye was now seeing double, he told me that I was lucky I was an artist, not a doctor. I said, sure, lucky I like Cubism."

He turned his bandaged eyes toward me.

"What if color never returns to my left eye? What if each eye sees a different world?"

"You'll paint diptychs," I said.

As soon as I got him into bed, he asked me to open the box of invitations that had arrived that morning. He took the card from my hand and held it up, as if he could see his doll sentries.

"How does it look?" he asked.

"Incredible," I said. "The colors are perfect."

Later that evening, feeding him his dinner, I asked, "How did you know which side of the card was front or back?"

"The varnish. Extra glossy on the image side."

I had printed the address labels beforehand this time, taking heed of my mother's warning and accepting the fact that Arnold's and my love was no more "dynamic and original" than anyone else's, that I got no special consideration for cruelty for being half his age.

Before his surgery, Arnold had completed another twenty works, while I had not written a single word. Sitting at my computer every morning from eight to noon had become commensurate with staring at myself in a magnifying mirror for four hours. How could I not find myself ugly?

The first night of Arnold's convalescence I slept on the sofa. Around midnight, I startled myself awake and went to check on him. I had forgotten to shut the bedroom light. Snoring loudly from the anesthesia, his bandaged eyes wrapped in thick gauze, he lay supine, unaware of my presence. I crossed the room and stood over him. He looked helpless and blind and unbearably old, and I feared that the most difficult part of my life was about to begin.

I returned to the sofa, but only slept in fits and starts.

When I checked on him the next morning, I found him sitting up in bed, labeling his invitations by touch alone.

"How are you feeling? Can I get you anything?" I asked.

"I think I've got everything I need. Go finish your novel."

How could I not return to my computer to try to chip away at the frozen improbable love story while my sixty-three-year-old husband was in the next room blindly labeling invitations to an exhibition that would open while he still wore bandages over his eyes?

22

ARNOLD'S DEALER, THE BOY WHO USED TO HAVE FLAMBOYANT
hair, was now covered with Kaposi lesions. We had gone to visit him
in the now closed gallery and found him in a froth of indignation. He
had just returned from the public pool after having been told he could
no longer use it. It was 1988. Arnold borrowed a pair of his swimming
briefs, and they walked back to the pool while I went home to retrieve
my bathing suit.

I only saw them again poolside. They stood at the deep end, the boy
gripping Arnold's arm to steady himself. Arnold was sixty-five, but next
to the boy, he looked robust. In fact, Arnold would go on to paint and
exhibit for another twenty-eight years. Our marriage was not yet half
over. But this boy was dying now.

From the far side of the pool, I could make out the purple lesions
on his face, chest, and legs. The swimmers could not exit the water fast
enough. The lifeguard blew his whistle.

Arnold took his dealer's hand and they jumped simultaneously,
making the biggest splash a skeletal boy and an old man could manage.
I never loved Arnold more.

23

WHICH BRINGS ME TO THE POINT IN OUR STORY WHEN I BEGAN *Half a Life,* 1993. I was forty, Arnold seventy.

I had finally finished my novel after four more arduous years of coaxing my characters forward. Maybe that was why the novel never felt wholly realized to me, though I published it anyway. Something about my characters—the teenage narrator and the older man—felt too fanciful for the sad ending, when the narrator, now in her forties, realizes how old her husband has become.

I hoped that by writing my story as nonfiction this time (drawing from memory rather than imagination, as if the two could be separated), I would be able to spend more time analyzing my characters' nuances rather than having to build them from scratch. The process would be closer to life drawing than to caricature, or so I believed.

As I mentioned earlier, *Half a Life* begins with my hardscrabble childhood under the dominion of my autistic father. Arnold does not appear until page 118, halfway through the manuscript.

He [the art teacher] was in his mid-forties, gray-templed, with a scruffy black beard and heavy square glasses like the kind Clark Kent wore to hide his otherworldly good looks.

I used to keep a captain's log of my daily output (why?), so I have a fair idea of when I wrote what. According to the log, I wrote that sentence during early December 1993, in my study on East 7th Street.

Arnold was in our bedroom, unable to go to his studio that winter. He was recuperating from a second bout of bronchitis in as many years. I always read him my morning's output, even if only a sentence, before heading off to teach. He was my first audience, as I was his first viewer.

Sitting on the edge of our bed, I read, "*On my last night of art class, I dawdled in the hall until the other students were finished. I heeled the wall and watched them file out. As soon as they were gone, I slipped back into the classroom and shut the door behind me. Arnold was leaning against a window frame, arms folded, eyes shut, yawning. This time I approached him without a hint of coyness, without the spark of a blush.*"

"I remember you coming up behind me and me turning around," he said, "but I'm not sure who kissed who first. I think I kissed you."

"*I unbuttoned the top three buttons of my peasant blouse, crossed the ink-splattered floor, and kissed him. He kissed me back, then stopped himself.*"

"I think you're right," Arnold said. "I think you kissed me first. I would have been scared shitless to kiss a seventeen-year-old."

"Sixteen," I said.

I read on, "*I asked him if he would sleep with me. He looked stunned. I mustered all my nerve and asked again. 'Maybe we should talk,' he said. I shook my head no. 'Sweetheart, I can't sleep with you. I'd like to, but I can't.'*"

"I would never have called you 'sweetheart.' You were my student," Arnold said. "And I don't think I would have looked 'stunned.' Maybe surprised at your boldness."

When Arnold made suggestions about how his character would act or what his character would say or not say, was it still my story? Were we not colluding? Had we become collaborators in the darker meaning of the word?

———

Had Arnold lived to read the pages I am now writing, what would he have made of them?

But in the last memoir, you said—you wrote—*that you kissed me.*

This is a reconsideration, I would have said.

All art is a reconsideration, he would have said.

Had Arnold experienced the sea change of the MeToo era, would he have come to believe that he crossed a line when he first kissed me?

Does a story's ending excuse its beginning?

Does a kiss in one moment mean something else entirely five decades later?

Can a love that starts with such an asymmetrical balance of power ever right itself?

———

Some writers hear voices dictating to them, others spy on their fellow mortals through a keyhole, while still others, like myself, worm into their protagonist's mind to stand sentry at the door of consciousness.

How do I convey yearning for a kiss while at the same time acknowledge the predatory act of an older man kissing a teenager? Perhaps had I been the type of writer who peeked at her characters through the keyhole, I would have seen a middle-aged man kissing an underage girl. I might have been repelled by what I saw and written a different scene. But I was inside the girl, yearning for the kiss.

I had intended to write the truth, the whole truth, and nothing but the truth, but I could not find it, or else I found it everywhere.

24

"I'M THE SAME AGE GOYA WAS WHEN HE PAINTED *THE DROWNING Dog*," Arnold said the midnight he turned seventy-three. We were seated on a park bench in Tompkins Square. It was full summer and too hot to stay in our apartment. "He was living at the farmhouse he had bought miles from Madrid. He had been going deaf for decades, but now he was stone deaf. Stone. What a perfect description. Think about it: He had once been the favored portraitist of the Spanish royal court, and now the only person who saw his work was the peasant woman who cleaned and cooked for him."

"Do you think she thought the dog was drowning or swimming?" I asked.

"She thought the dog was going to heaven either way."

Arnold's appreciation of Goya had evolved over time from reverence of a master to camaraderie with another septuagenarian. Arnold had finally accepted that the power of the Black Paintings could not be separated from the medium in which they grew, the coming solitude of old age.

Arnold had been alone in one studio or another for nearly half a century.

The studios had changed, but not the loneliness of struggling and arguing with himself unobserved. His dealer and the twenty-something East Village artists, the exuberant boys and girls who had visited his studio and danced with him at the Palladium, had perished of AIDS or overdoses or moved on to Soho galleries. Neo-Expressionism fell out of favor. The colors of Arnold's palette—crimson, Venetian red, Mars black, burnt sienna, yellow ochre, cobalt blue—were replaced by inkjet colors. Then painting itself, the human mark, the fallibility of touch, fell out of favor.

"Am I out of my mind to continue painting?" Arnold would ask as he continued to paint. "I'm like a medieval monk working on an illuminated manuscript after the printing press was invented."

Before he would prepare his palette for the day, refill the buckets of water, rinse out his sponges and submerge his brushes for one last cleanse, he would turn off his hearing aids and leave them in his ears. The dead plugs further muffled the outside world. His studio was on Avenue B and 2nd Street, the last corner holdout of the East Village heroin trade. From his always open window (to disperse the formaldehyde fumes in acrylic paint), he saw a man shot down, a woman overdose, a police raid where a stray bullet killed a Pomeranian while it did its business on the curb. He only closed the window the day after 9/11 to ward off an even more nauseating stench than formaldehyde: burning bodies.

He painted—not the hellscape that was outside his window, but the hellscape that was eternal, the same view that Goya had.

No matter the hour, whenever I stopped by his studio unannounced, I would find him working. We had his palette table put on casters to give him more mobility and freedom. When he thought I wasn't looking, he would lean on the table, as if it were a walker, and push himself toward his painting. Whenever his age overcame me and I would be on the brink of heartbreak, the stroke his brush left behind on the canvas would be no less muscular and vibrant than it had ever been.

I came to believe what Goya's housekeeper must have believed each time she returned from the butcher and saw the old master feverishly painting day after week after month: She was witnessing a miracle.

25

HOW DOES ONE GROW OLD AS THE YOUNGER WOMAN? ONE
doesn't. I always looked fresher than he. If I gained a few pounds, he
gained more. If my skin wasn't as taut as it once was, his was looser.
And I always had more energy. When he fell asleep during a movie, I
poked him awake. When he nodded off during a dinner party, I kicked
him under the table. As his senses diminished, mine grew keener. From
ten yards off, I could spot a crack in the sidewalk before he stumbled.
From another room, I could hear the punch lines to jokes he missed on
TV and shout them back to him. Arnold still retained his impressive,
curious mind, but he lost things daily—keys, words, height, mass, the
ability to hear conversations. And most alarming, the loss of the sixth
sense, proprioception, the ability to know the position of one's body
parts. Arnold wasn't always sure where his hands and feet were without having to look for them. It took him a wooden moment to reach
for things, to make those measurements one unconsciously calculates
each time one dips under a low beam or eats popcorn in the dark. I
was becoming his copilot. My senses worked double time shepherding
his body and mine through space, but not to point out the cracked

sidewalk, not to repeat the punch line he couldn't hear, would mean abandoning him in the wooly, dim, mute isolation of old age.

Were my acts selfless, or was this the price I was willing to pay for my own eternal youth—to always be the younger woman? After all, I suspected that my Shangri-la would vanish upon his death and I would become old overnight.

26

WHEN THE SMOKE FROM THE BURNING HOLE WHERE THE WORLD Trade Center once stood made Arnold's bronchitis worse, and our four-flight walk-up became too taxing for him, I took a teaching job in Central Florida.

I was fifty, Arnold eighty.

With the proceeds from our East Village walk-up, we bought a mid-century glass house at the end of a dirt road (near the university where I would be teaching) and built Arnold a studio with a view of a wild lake. Alligators basking on the shore replaced drug dealers lurking on the corner. The studio, his twenty-third, was his largest to date, with a whole separate wing of floor-to-ceiling painting racks, enough to comfortably hold fifty-five years of productivity.

The evening we finished moving the paintings into their new barracks, after the workers left, we stood by his wall of glass and watched the sky and the lake become one.

I waited for him to say something about what had happened earlier that day when the sixty-foot semitrailer truck containing his life's work had first pulled into the dirt driveway. He had cried (I had only seen him cry once before, and that was for his daughter), and when I asked him why, he apologized for burdening me with his life's work.

"If you look closely at the lake," he said, "you can see that the colors in the reflection are the opposite of the colors in real life. The sky above the tree line is a cold yellow with streaks of viridian, but its reflection in the lake is a warm orange with streaks of magenta. It will take me some time to figure out this palette. Titian was right when he said the artist learns color last. Do you know what his last words were at ninety-nine?"

I did not.

"If I only had ten more years, then, maybe, maybe I'd know what I am doing."

As Arnold waited to understand this new landscape, he completed the last pages of an illuminated manuscript he had been working on for the past three years. As monks once illustrated the Bible with gold leaf and devotion, he was illuminating the 760-page file that the FBI had kept on him from October 5, 1945, until early 1972. Just before we moved to Florida, Arnold had been rediscovered yet again by a new generation of artists and curators. The first volume of his illuminated manuscript had been exhibited at MoMA PS1 (his first museum show in New York), and the attention and accolades made him less fearful of moving to Central Florida and being forgotten.

Sending away for his FBI file had been my idea. When the Freedom of Information Act declassified the Cold War documents, I requested his—a birthday surprise. I reasoned that one of us could use what was in those papers for our work. When he opened the box stamped *FBI Confidential,* and flipped through the redacted pages, he said, "A school could have been built for what it cost to spy on me."

At first, he had read the pages as if they were entries he had kept in a forgotten journal.

October 12, 1946, neighbor was interviewed telephonically. She was most cooperative and expressed great admiration for the FBI.

She told agent that subjects' trash pail contained remnants of a banner against the A-bomb.

Which neighbor?

December 10, 1960, an informant observed the subject has a hernia scar on his right side and no other distinguishing marks.

Which lover?

The beauty of the pages began to captivate him. The sheets came blacked out, or partially obscured, all the names but his shrouded. What remained was sheer abstraction, the very shapes of subterfuge, the silhouettes of duplicity. The idea of illustrating the actual files came to him months later in a used bookshop. He saw a copy of an illuminated manuscript and knew instantly how he'd utilize those pages. In place of crosses and saints, martyrs and angels, he'd paint A-bombs, Mouseketeers, two-tone refrigerators, Khrushchev and Nixon. Instead of ornate, delicate gold-leaf borders, he'd stencil on the perforated patterns of vintage 1950s paper doilies. Instead of the Bible's Psalms, he'd copy the FBI's accusations.

While Arnold completed the last pages of his illuminated manuscript, I began a novel about an artist who was illustrating his FBI dossier. Of course the novel was about more than that, but what interests us here is that the character, whom I named Alex, was not *like* Arnold; he *was* Arnold. I gave him Arnold's height, weight, blood pressure, medicines, temperament, principles, and background. The only change I made was to give him a wife his own age. I was curious—more than curious—compelled to learn who Arnold might have become without me.

As the novel opens, Alex and Ruth, both in their late seventies, prepare to sell their home of forty-five years, an East Village walk-up. As I always did, I read Arnold the pages as I wrote them. We usually sat on the deck under a three-hundred-year-old live oak adorned with Spanish moss. After thirty years in an apartment, the novelty of sitting outdoors enchanted us. As he once listened to my words over traffic, he now tried to hear them over chirping insects.

I read, "*Alex and Ruth were being wrenched away from everything they loved and knew just when their age demanded stability. Alex gently closed the ancient entry door behind them (lest the old glass break before their open house tomorrow) and took hold of the railing (lest he slip on the icy steps).*"

"You're making him too pathetic," Arnold said. "He's too frail and cautious. Why do writers always make old people feeble? It's a cliché."

"*And for the first time since Alex signed the Realtor's contract three days ago, the heady intoxication returned. Even if they couldn't afford Manhattan, with a million dollars, they could afford just about anywhere else—the Jersey shore, or that car-less island in North Carolina he saw advertised in* The New Yorker, *or Fort Myers close to Ruth's sister. But he didn't want to be banished to Florida, where it was too hot to walk and neither of them had ever learned to drive.*"

"And why do you have to make him frightened of change?" Arnold asked. "I wasn't scared to move to Florida. Who is this guy?"

"He is you," I said. "You if you'd married someone your own age."

27

THE SECRET LIFE OF THE YOUNGER WOMAN. WE ALWAYS RECOG-
nized one another. The well-put-together fifty-something wife helping
her elderly husband into a taxi as I helped Arnold out of one. Our eyes
locked. There was a natural curiosity—a fascination, really—about
others of our kind, how they were faring as their husbands aged. And
there was a certain jealousy among us, almost a schadenfreude. *Mine
might use a cane, but yours uses a walker.* But there was also kindness,
like the evening a widow (her husband had been twenty-eight years
older than she) took me aside at a dinner party to tell me not to waste
my time rehearsing grief; I would never get it right.

One afternoon, a few months after we moved to Florida, Arnold
and I were dining near the campus when I noticed an attractive girl,
twenty at most, studying us. I knew she had been watching us because
she looked embarrassed when I caught her attention. The man who
shared her booth was about my age, fifty, old enough to be her father,
but as a younger woman myself, I knew he wasn't her father as she knew
Arnold wasn't mine.

Later, she and I ran into each other in the ladies' room. Her curious
glance seemed to seek something from me, but one can never be sure.

What did she want to ask me? Do I have regrets? Was it worth it? Or maybe she wanted more practical advice. Does he often not get hard? Are you in his will? Is the condo in your name? What do you do about his children who are older than you?

As she silently left the bathroom, she turned around to stare at me again. I finally recognized her expression—an amalgamation of fear and awe. The girl wasn't seeking my advice. I was about her age when I, too, saw my first *old* younger woman.

28

I WAS SO SADDENED BY MY MOTHER'S NEWS THAT I COULD NOT call up the words *chronic* or *acute*. Instead, I asked, "Is it the good kind or the bad kind?"

"No one told me there was a good kind," my mother said. Only minutes before, she had been told that she had late-stage leukemia, that she might only have months, maybe weeks. She phoned me from her car outside her doctor's office. She had been so cavalier about the appointment that she insisted Gene, her third husband, not accompany her. Now she was alone in her Mercedes-Benz, the icon of her earthly success, talking to her daughter on the far side of the continent. She sounded breathless, as if she had sprinted across the parking lot.

She said, "Do you know what Dr. Foxx suggested after he gave me the oncologist's number? He told me that I could choose not to fight and enjoy the time I have left, that I should factor in my age." She was eighty. "Can you imagine?"

Still reeling and unable to control my anguish, I grunted affirmatively to let her know that I shared her umbrage at being told she was mortal.

I said, "Dr. Foxx was only trying to give you options."

"To do nothing? Is Arnold there?" she interrupted me. "I need to talk to him," she said.

When Arnold picked up the extension, she told him what she had told me, that Dr. Foxx had said that she should factor in her age. "He implied I was too old to fight."

"You're only eighty," Arnold said. He had just turned eighty-six. "Of course you're going to fight with every drug in the arsenal."

So that is what he will want when the time comes, I thought.

We flew to Los Angeles the next day. (My brothers and I staggered our visits so that one of us would always be with her.) She was waiting for Arnold and me by the front gate. In the months since I had last seen her, her face had fossilized into an old woman's. I don't know who was more disturbed by the other's appearance. I watched her face as Arnold emerged from the taxi's back seat, cane tip first, tentatively tapping the curb for purchase, a flash of compression socks, and then an agonized groan from deep within his diaphragm as he used his cane to hoist himself off the seat's ledge and then vault himself over the curb. He hugged my mother and she squeezed him back.

Later that afternoon, each took me aside to express shock at the other's appearance. Each feared for me the loss I would experience after the other's death. Each warned me to take care of myself first, not to allow caretaking to consume me, then asked for a glass of water or a pillow or a pencil that dropped.

As I did the dinner dishes that evening, a sixth sense compelled me to look out the patio screen door. My mother and Arnold reclined side by side on lawn chairs, staring up at the night sky.

"Do you know what worries me most," she told Arnold. "That for the remainder of my life, my only thoughts will be about death, that I will no longer be able to wonder what I want for dinner without the death bell tolling."

"I hear that bell all the time. I thought it was the dinner bell," Arnold said.

My mother laughed.

They would have made an interesting couple.

Michelle was supposed to visit while we were in Los Angeles, but she phoned to say that her psychiatrist thought the visit might be too stressful. Her own mother had died a few years before, and Michelle had been her caretaker. She still lived in the North Hollywood house. She still kept her clothes in her childhood closet and slept in her childhood bed.

I was about to hang up the extension in the living room when I heard Michelle say, "I have cancer, too, Dad."

"What kind?"

"Blood."

"Leukemia?"

"I'm still having tests."

"For leukemia?"

"And other stuff."

"When do you get the results?"

"I have an appointment with my chiropractor this week."

"Your chiropractor?"

I cradled the receiver. Michelle did not have cancer and I could not bear to listen as she dropped her enigmatic clues that sent her father on another scavenger hunt for the truth.

My mother sat drinking a bottle of Ensure. Gene poured me and himself a cup of coffee. When Arnold finally joined us at the kitchen table, he looked as if he had been gone years and had returned a changed man.

"She says she might have leukemia, that she's waiting for test results. What if she's telling the truth this time?"

I said, "You don't think it is a little coincidental that she's diagnosed—by a chiropractor, mind you—with the same disease as my mom on the day we arrive? You talked to her last night for over an hour, you don't think she would have mentioned it?"

Arnold pressed his palms against his eyelids and allowed himself a short cry in front of Gene and my mother. After composing himself and accepting Gene's offer of coffee, he said, "I don't even know if I love her anymore. I know I feel responsibility for her and sorrow, but is that the same as love?"

"I used to believe that I would never stop loving my boys," Gene said, whose two sons had not spoken to him in decades after a violent, acrimonious divorce during which his wife gutshot him. "And that's true, I never did. But they are men in their fifties now. I don't love those men and I don't want to pretend that I do. I feel for you, I do. I think I'm the luckier father. I can't imagine what my adult sons are like. I never think of them except as boys, and I allow myself to love those boys. A couple of years ago, I saw my younger son coming out of a 7-Eleven. He's a fat middle-aged man I wouldn't recognize except that he has his mother's face. Am I supposed to love that?"

Arnold abruptly stood. "I'm going to call Michelle and demand that she tell me the truth right now."

"Sit down," my mother said. "She doesn't have leukemia. If she wants cancer, she can have mine."

While I packed and arranged for a taxi to return us to the airport, Arnold and my mother took a walk along the bay to say good-bye. When they did not return after a half hour, I went to look for them. They only had one cane between them. They were not on the bay side of the peninsula, so I went to the ocean side, where the sand was deeper and the sea more treacherous. The boardwalk was congested with bikes and skateboards and tourists. I searched a quarter mile in each direction, then headed for the pier. On the far end, where the fishermen congregate, I finally spotted them, but they did not see me. My mother grasped the pier railing with one hand and Arnold's arm with the other, while Arnold used his cane to keep them upright. To anyone on the pier that morning, they were an old married couple still devoted to each other.

29

TWO WEEKS BEFORE THE FILMING WAS TO BEGIN, I LEARNED that my novel *Heroic Measures,* published five years before, the one about the old couple selling their apartment, was going to be made into a movie starring Morgan Freeman as Arnold and Diane Keaton as his age-appropriate wife.

The novel had been optioned by a small independent production company soon after it was published, but I hardly put stock in a movie being made from such unlikely material.

The producer, embarrassed that no one had told me the movie was being made, rushed the screenplay to the Brooklyn summer sublet that Arnold and I had rented to escape the Florida heat.

Reading the adaptation of my novel was not exactly like reading a pathology report, but the tension was similar. It took a few scenes before I could hear my internal reading voice over my banging pulse. The sensation of hearing myself read another person's version of my story felt akin to confiding a dream to a distracted therapist who then gets all the facts wrong as he misinterprets it.

I felt queasy and thirsty. Arnold brought me a glass of water.

Finally, I recognized a few lines of dialogue taken verbatim from my novel, an exchange between Alex and Ruth of which I was particularly fond. It was like seeing my eyes looking back at me from another person's face.

When I finished reading, Arnold asked, "One star or five?"

I handed him the screenplay and watched his face as he read. After a few pages, I could tell that he was spellbound. He was no longer the frail Alex I described in the novel; he was now Morgan Freeman, fourteen years younger and a foot higher.

When Arnold finished reading, I asked, "What the hell is it about?"

Arnold said, "Remember what that Hollywood producer told Joan Didion when she asked him what her adaptation was about? 'It is about two movie stars!'"

We were invited to have brunch with Morgan and the producers the following weekend at a private dining room in an Upper West Side hotel that Morgan frequented. The waitstaff knew to treat him attentively but not sycophantically. Before the food arrived, Morgan asked Arnold to show him how an artist, not a hobbyist, held a paintbrush, approached a canvas, applied paint.

Arnold rose from his chair. At eighty-nine, it took him a couple of tries. His hip barely cleared the table. He was now three inches shorter than me. When we kissed, I had to bend down.

While Morgan watched, Arnold reached for a fork as if it were a brush, held it tightly by its neck, mashed the tines against the white tablecloth as if it were a palette, and then applied imaginary paint to an imaginary canvas. His strokes were fluid as he dipped and jabbed.

"Are you always in motion while you paint?" Morgan asked.

"It's a dance," Arnold said.

After the food arrived, I watched Morgan study Arnold and subtly mimic the way Arnold stabbed his fork into his eggs, the gusto with which Arnold chewed.

When Arnold finally grew aware of Morgan's embodiment of him,

Arnold smiled and said, "I thought all we had in common was gray hair."

Morgan smiled back. "I always wanted to play a Jew," he said.

———

The interior sets for Alex and Ruth's apartment (essentially a replica of our old East Village walk-up) had been fabricated inside a cavernous soundstage in the Brooklyn Navy Yard. The day before filming was to begin, Arnold and I were invited by the art director to visit the sets, a maze of three-dimensional interiors. The rooms looked much as I had described them in the novel—a prewar warren cluttered with books and artwork. For the artwork, the art director had borrowed Arnold's paintings. Entering the set felt almost as if we were walking through the rooms of our old apartment on East 7th Street, but something felt off. There was too much nostalgia in the decor, too many mementos on the shelves. Only when I noticed an open book on Ruth's bedroom nightstand and read the inscription—*To Ruth, Happy 1st Anniversary, Love Alex, 1953*—did it hit me. That was my birth year. This was the home of a couple who had grown old together.

———

On the first day of filming, Arnold was offered a director's chair with an unobstructed view of the set for Alex's studio. I was too anxious to sit. In the scene about to be filmed, Alex is working on a large expressionist portrait of Ruth. Arnold had finished the portrait of Diane Keaton only yesterday.

As Morgan reached for a brush and approached the canvas, I looked over at Arnold, precariously perched on the edge of his chair. His frailty was now the first thing that people noticed about him, not his personhood or his charm or his impressive mind. He wore orthopedic shoes, and his feet dangled just shy of the footrest, but his eyes were bright with amazement. Morgan Freeman was playing him as young again, only in his mid-seventies, vibrant, dancing as he painted.

An hour before the movie's premiere at the Toronto Film Festival, Arnold discovered that his pants were too long. When he came out of our hotel bathroom, the hems dragged on the rug. He had shrunk another inch since he bought the suit two years before to wear to his one hundredth solo show.

I had never learned to sew. My mother used a stapler to hem her children's clothes. I borrowed one from the front desk and practiced the art as my mother had taught me—staple from the inside out, the small metal legs, not the crown, showing.

As Arnold stepped back into his newly hemmed pants, a protruding staple scratched his ankle bone. Of late, his skin had become so thin and friable that the slightest cut would bleed profusely. I stanched the flow with tissue and pressure, then taped the wound closed with butterfly Band-Aids we had brought for just such an emergency. I helped him put on his compression socks and orthopedic shoes, and then tied the laces for him.

We were now late. As I waited impatiently for him to find his cane, I did a quick assessment of myself in the room's full-length mirror. I was wearing my best outfit, a pantsuit I bought at an Eileen Fisher outlet, which now looked matronly and grim to me. My weaker eyelid drooped. I hadn't slept well in days. I dreaded public speaking, and the producers had asked me to go onstage for the Q and A after the premiere.

But no matter what I looked like, I was still the younger woman.

The publicist instructed Arnold and me how to "walk the red carpet." As we stepped onto the carpet, we were to turn toward the half dozen or so photographers covering the film's premiere. It was raining, so the red carpet had been tented. As the cameras snapped, we were supposed to face the first photographer, smile, turn slightly, face the next, smile, and so on and so on. Arnold needed his cane and my arm to manage. I was sixty, Arnold ninety.

As I helped him up the stairs to reach our seats in the reserved section of the theater, Arnold said, "This was the best summer of my life."

30

I WAS NOT WITH ARNOLD WHEN HE LEARNED THAT HE WAS dying. Neither of us had suspected that anything was especially wrong with him when he left for the doctor's that morning. I mean, at ninety-three, something was always wrong with him, but we could no longer distinguish between the new wrongs and the old.

I had not gone with him to the doctor's because I had reached a difficult point in the novel I was writing and did not want to break my momentum. I had to decide how one of my principal characters—the husband—would die. All I knew was that his death would be from natural causes. I had made him eighty-six years old, so I had a wide array of choices. In the chapter I was struggling with, the husband simultaneously learns that he is dying and that his younger wife, fifty-two, has cheated on him.

The day before the doctor's visit, Arnold had asked me how I was going to kill the old guy in this book.

"Heart attack," I mused.

"Too fast," Arnold said. "All you will be left with is the wife's grief. The drama will become too internal. What you need instead is a slow impending death, but not too slow, a chance for a few more scenes between the husband and wife."

"I guess cancer is the obvious choice," I said.

"But what kind?" Arnold asked.

"Brain?"

Arnold shook his head. "The reader might think that what the husband does and says is the result of his disease. That takes away his free will. Is that what you want the story to be about?"

"Pancreatic?"

"You'll think of something."

In fact, that morning in his doctor's office, Arnold learned that he (and my character) would be dying of acute myeloid leukemia, the same disease that had killed my mother five years before.

———

I turned on my phone around noon and saw that Arnold had left a dozen messages. Before I could listen to them, the phone rang again.

"Arnold?" I answered.

"This is Dr. Horwitz," said a concerned male voice. "My nurse has been trying to reach you. I'm afraid the news isn't good. Your husband has leukemia."

"Tell her the prognosis," I heard Arnold say in the background.

"Your husband wants me to tell you the prognosis," said the doctor. "It's a very aggressive cancer."

"How aggressive?" I asked.

"There is no way to predict without a bone marrow biopsy."

"And what would that tell us?"

"Whether he has weeks or months."

"There's nothing experimental, a trial?"

"Not at his age."

Arnold was sitting right there, listening.

"May I talk to him?"

"Hello, who is this?" Arnold asked.

"Me."

"Did he tell you my prognosis?"

He was asleep on a plastic chair in the crowded waiting area when I arrived at the doctor's. Head back, mouth open, he looked more unconscious than napping.

I knelt before him and put my head on his lap.

He opened his eyes. "I'm dying," he said.

"I'm so sorry you had to hear this alone," I said.

"I'm very discouraged," he said.

"The doctor said you could have months."

"Only months?"

He slept all the way home. As I struggled to get him into bed, he said, "I always thought I would die in my sleep, just not wake up one day."

"That's because you're an optimist," I said.

Later that evening, as I put away the dinner he did not touch, I heard him crying in our bedroom for the third time in his life, this time for himself.

I gave him his privacy until the sobs subsided. He had every right to cry for what was about to be taken from him.

Everything.

When I finally joined him in the bedroom, he said, "It's hard to believe that I'm not going to be here in a few weeks."

"You could have months," I said.

"It's just as impossible to accept that I'm not going to be here in a few months," he said.

I could not think of a response because there was none.

The next morning, he was back in his studio.

When he saw me standing in the doorway, staring at him, speechless, he said, "You should be taking notes for your book."

With only weeks to live, he found mixing colors too time-consuming. His last drawing was a pen-and-ink landscape—the lake and the woods beyond. Rather than draw the woods as a solid black shape, he drew the trees individually. He was getting weaker by the day and there were thousands of trees. Did he hope that as long as there were trees still to be drawn, he would be allowed to finish?

He drew the trees as thick, black, nuanced lines running from the top of the paper to the horizon, a pencil line. From the horizon to the bottom of the paper, he drew the trees' less stable gray reflections in the lake.

He worked long hours for a man who was dying. He returned to his studio every morning, if only to sleep in his armchair.

Just shy of total blackness, while a few bright shafts of white paper remained, he put away his pen and ink and asked me to help him back to bed, which he never again left.

Despite the drawing's dense geometric bars of darkness, its lack of a vanishing point, it does not read as flat. The untouched paper—the shafts of "sunlight"—allude to a dazzling meadow beyond the trees, a place you could reach if only your imagination allowed.

Who did Arnold imagine was on the far side of the trees? His mother and father? Goya and Orozco? The boy with flamboyant hair? Our beloved dachshund? His mother-in-law and confidante?

31

"I WANT YOU TO HELP ME DESTROY THE PAINTINGS I THINK ARE failures," he said as he lay dying. Earlier that day, the hospice nurse had told us he had days now, not weeks.

"Help me to my studio and I'll show you which ones." He sat up in bed, unaided. "I can't believe I'm going to die," he said.

Before I helped him stand, I asked, "Sweetheart, do you really want to spend your last weeks destroying your work?"

"Days, the nurse said. Yes," he said adamantly.

"How?"

"Burn them."

"Tonight? Where? In our backyard?"

"Use a box cutter. Slash an *X* through them."

"You might change your mind."

"When? Next week?"

I helped him to his studio and turned his armchair around so that instead of facing the lake, it now faced his life's work. He refused the chair and asked me to help him walk closer to his work. He was alert in a way I had not seen him in days. The film of opacity that had blighted his vision all but washed away with his rapid blinking.

He wanted to start with the largest paintings. "Pull them out of the racks one at a time, not all the way, only a few inches, enough so that I recognize the palette."

I did as he asked.

Cadmium orange and Venetian red.

Success, failure?

Burnt sienna and raw umber.

Exceptional, mediocre?

Phthalo blue and viridian.

Valuable, worthless?

Yellow ochre and Mars violet.

Deep, shallow?

Mars black and titanium white.

Timeless, expired?

"Take me back to bed," he said. "Only wake me when it's over."

After he fell asleep, unable to bear another minute of listening for his last breath as I sobbed, I returned to the racks to assess what awaited me. The culling of his work would be our last collaboration. I started looking through the paintings. Success, failure? Success, failure? What does that even mean?

Then I saw the first portrait he had painted of me. *Jill #1.*

How did he see me at seventeen? He had rendered me in the composition of a Renaissance maiden. A plumb line runs from my forehead to my clavicle. The shadow and light of contrapposto zigzags down my profile. The viewer's eye can't resist leaping from one triangle of light to another. He underpainted my flesh tones with vermilion so that a pink blush radiates from under my skin. The strokes that make up my hair strands become the strokes that give my face contour, depth. But the most striking detail is my closed eyes.

Are they closed in trust? Or am I refusing to see?

I had never been painted before when Arnold had asked me to sit for him the first time. (He had not yet left his wife for me, but he had recently told me that he loved me.) My elation made sitting still difficult. I had to close my eyes to quiet my nerves, and as I did, Arnold had told me to hold that pose.

I shut the studio lights and went to check on him, asleep in our bed, in a puddle of lamplight, his arm dangling over the side—the same position he was in when I went to seduce him forty-five years before.

I crossed the room and stood over him. He stirred and opened his eyes. There might be a dispute about our first kiss, but there could be none about our last.

ACKNOWLEDGMENTS

I am especially grateful to the following people for reading early drafts and providing insights that helped immensely with the book: Jo Ann Beard, Alan Brown, Susan Burton, RL Goldberg, Amy Hempel, Gail Hochman, Nicole Holofcener, David Leavitt, Ann Patty, and Victoria Wilson.

A NOTE ON THE TYPE

This book was set in Adobe Garamond. Designed for the Adobe Corporation by Robert Slimbach, the fonts are based on types first cut by Claude Garamond (ca. 1480–1561). Garamond was a pupil of Geoffroy Tory and is believed to have followed the Venetian models, although he introduced a number of important differences, and it is to him that we owe the letter we now know as "old style." He gave to his letters a certain elegance and feeling of movement that won their creator an immediate reputation and the patronage of Francis I of France.

Composed by North Market Street Graphics
Lancaster, Pennsylvania

Printed and bound by Berryville Graphics
Berryville, Virginia

Designed by Casey Hampton